Every Marriage is Different

RUTHANN RIDLEY

D1416765

VICTOR BOOKS

A DIVISION OF SCRIPTURE PRESS PUBLICATIONS INC.
USA CANADA ENGLAND

Editor: Carolyn Nystrom
Cover Design: Mardelle Ayres
Cover Photo: William Koechling

Recommended Dewey Decimal Classification: 248.4
Suggested Subject Heading: PERSONAL RELIGION: MARRIAGE

Library of Congress Catalog Card Number: 92-061794
ISBN: 1-56476-051-0

1 2 3 4 5 6 7 8 9 10 Printing/Year 97 96 95 94 93

VICTOR BOOKS
A Division of SP Publications, Inc.
Wheaton, Illinois 60187

CONTENTS

INTRODUCTION

At the core of each of us lives a holy passion to love and be loved. We long for a bridegroom who will love us perfectly. We dream of being able to love a man with a vibrant, unbreakable love. These yearnings are memories, imprints perhaps, of the perfect relationship God intended when He designed marriage.

Marriage has fallen far short of God's original plan. Today in marriage we come to each other confused, sin-layered, and sometimes frantic to achieve the love and harmony for which we long. We labor under many misconceptions. One of those misconceptions is the idea that if we model our marriage on another marriage that seems ideal, all of our problems will be solved.

They won't. Every marriage is different. If you put two unique personalities together, the resulting marriage personality will also be unique.

This book is designed to help you discover the personality of your marriage and what will work for you. We will be exploring ten marriages in the Bible, all real, all human. Some of the husbands and wives are quite ordinary. Others are people of great faith. But every one of their marriages is different.

Since marriage is a mutual affair, this book is designed to draw husbands into the learning process. Each chapter includes ideas for one-on-one husband and wife discussion about concepts such as:

- 🐞 the cultivation of space for listening and growing
- 🐞 the kind of leadership a woman most easily follows
- 🐞 the experience of God's sufficiency in our marriage struggles
- 🐞 the "how" of learning to love in new ways

From Elizabeth and Zechariah, Priscilla and Aquila we learn that there are different kinds of unity.

From Isaac and Rebekah we learn the dangers of battling a husband's passiveness in ways that forget faith.

From Abigail, the wife of Nabal, we learn how to face the truth about a difficult husband and not become bitter.

From Abraham and Sarah we learn a healthy give-and-take. They were distinct individuals and yet they were one: bound up with one another, sending-receiving, receiving-sending, listening-responding, making allowances for one another. Their top priority in marriage was to be sensitive to the other's heart.

For each of you who studies this book, I pray a similar give-and-take and a similar richness within the complexity that is *your unique marriage.*

USING THIS STUDY GUIDE

This study is designed to be used in a group. But you can also use it for personal study or as a study for husband and wife. Each chapter has five sections:

Lessons from the Marriage of . . . : A question and answer study based on a passage of Scripture about a marriage in the Bible. This study includes application questions for your own marriage.

Exploring Your Uniqueness: A choice of journal activities to help you sort through the issues of your own marriage. (These are personal and need not be shared.)

Interpreting the Data: A narrative section that discusses the underlying theme of the biblical marriage (Being Yourself, Communication, Unity, . . .). This section includes illustrations from contemporary marriages, quotations, and a verse for personal meditation.

Pathfinding with Your Husband: Ideas for activities with your husband, such as discussing a quote over dessert, making a chart, reflecting on a poem, setting parental goals.

Guiding the Study: A section at the back of the book with general guidelines for leading a group of women in this study, specific guides for each chapter, and field-tested ideas for a discussion party involving both husbands and wives.

GIVING YOUR SPOUSE A NAME
The Importance of Being Yourself in Marriage

LESSONS FROM THE MARRIAGE OF MANOAH AND HIS WIFE

Her husband was an important official in the community; she was a former beauty queen. But she loved her husband and liked to make him feel special. So she spent much of her time cooking gourmet meals, working in the vegetable garden, and beautifying their small home. Every evening after supper they discussed the issues the council had debated that day. Her husband valued her input and that meant a great deal. But deep inside she longed to be somebody in her own right. It was a desire she was afraid to share.

Everyone Is Someone

1. Read Judges 13. What overall impression do you get:

🍂 of Manoah?

🍂 of his wife?

🍂 of their marriage?

2. Record each phrase in the chapter that contains some reference to name or naming.

Verse   Phrase

3. How do you feel when someone fails to call you by name?

Everything in God's Word has a purpose. No detail, no mood, no omission is an accident. With this in mind, why do you think Manoah's wife is never given a name? (Record any idea.)

4. How might the concept of submission (Ephesians 5:21-22) be distorted and cause a wife in any century to feel like a nonperson?

5. How did God let Manoah's wife know she was special in His eyes? Consider the announcements and assurances in Genesis 17:15-17; 18:1-3, 8-10; 1 Samuel 1:9-18; Luke 1:8-17, 26-33.

Her Personality; His Personality

6. What can you tell about Manoah's wife's needs and personality from the following verses: Judges 13:2, 6, 9-10, 20-24?

7. Review the woman's account in Judges 13:6. Then write a sentence (more if it seems like fun) describing how you think the angel looked and how Manoah's wife might have responded to his presence. (Imagine how you would respond in her place.)

8. What do the following verses indicate about Manoah's personality: Judges 13:8-9, 11-12, 15-17, 20-22?

9. Manoah's name means "a resting place." How do you think he might have been a resting place for his wife?

Circle the words that best describe how you feel when you are with someone who accepts you just as you are (or initial the words with colored pens or draw a happy face or a flower beside them).

tense	free
nervous	sad
excited	relaxed
anxious	happy

10. How would you rate your acceptance of your husband on a scale of 1 to 10? 1 is low, 10 high. (This is for your eyes only.)

1 2 3 4 5 6 7 8 9 10

His acceptance of you?

1 2 3 4 5 6 7 8 9 10

How They Worked Together

11. a. Look again at Judges 13. Record the different places where you find the words *we* or *us*.

    b. What other hints of unity do you see in the relationship between Manoah and his wife? (Reread Judges 13:6-11, 21-23.)

12. How did her different view allow her to minister to him? (Judges 13:20-23)

How did his view allow him to minister to her? (vv. 9-12, 19-20)

13. Read Ephesians 4:15-16 in two or three translations. How might these verses apply to a Christian marriage?

14. What "otherness" in your husband is a help to you?

EXPLORING YOUR UNIQUENESS

On a separate sheet:
- ❦ Make a list of your own interests, abilities, and strengths. Then list your weaknesses.
- ❦ Do the same for your husband.
- ❦ Choose *one* of the following activities:
  –Write a paragraph about your husband's dreams and/or yours. (Or make a list and discuss it with your husband.)
  –If you had trouble with question 14, write about a day in your husband's life from his perspective.
  –Journal about differences that cause conflict or hurt between you. Write honestly. If you'd rather people didn't see the result, tear it up. Sometimes journaling can be as helpful as a session of counseling.

INTERPRETING THE DATA

The story of Manoah and his wife startles us with the truth that wives were far more than extensions of their husbands even in ancient cultures. They were individuals in their own right—valued and used by God.

Everyone is someone. Yet we all have times in our lives when we feel as if we are no one. In his letters to his brother, Theo, artist Vincent Van Gogh lamented that everybody seemed to shun him because he was different. He said, "There may be a great fire in our soul, and no one ever comes to warm himself at it; the passers-by see only a little bit of smoke coming through the chimney, and pass on their way."[1]

Once there was a young girl who lived in constant fear that she would do or say the wrong thing. She knew that she wasn't ugly, except a little. And she wasn't dumb, except in daily things that seemed to matter so much to everyone else—like fixing bicycle tires, or curling her hair in neat little rolls, or cooking without being messy, or remembering her dad's new phone number at work.

She tried to be good at these things, but she simply wasn't a practical kind of person. She would much rather have spent all her time drawing or writing poems. But her parents and peers saw little value in the arts. After she was married, she sensed that her husband also wanted her to be more practical. As years passed, she became discouraged and depressed. But she still believed that in order to be somebody, instead of nobody, she had to continue to pretend, to try to be the person other people wanted her to be.

What if Van Gogh had approached life in this way? He was pressured from every quarter to stop painting and go into a more "useful" vocation. What if he had listened? How impoverished we would be!

Being Yourself

Our unique interests, temperaments, and talents were fashioned by God. In the body of Christ every joint, every muscle, every nerve and ligament needs to perform the function for which it has aptitude. If it doesn't, the church will suffer. And so it is in that part of the body of Christ we call the Christian marriage. We need to allow our husbands to be themselves and they need to allow us to be ourselves, if we are going to be able to minister to each other in the way God planned.

In the biographical movie *My Left Foot*, Christy Brown's mother had her own passion, her own sense of what she and her husband needed to do for their son who was born with a severe case of cerebral palsy. Despite scarcely having money to buy food and coal, she saved bits of change so that they could buy a wheelchair for Christy. When it became clear that Christy had a profound artistic gift, his mother decided that he should have a room of his own in order to develop his talent. One day her husband came home to find his wife moving, stacking, and mortaring bricks. Challenged and a little shamed, he recruited the help of his other sons and finished the room himself.

Christy's mother was a woman who loved God. She understood

11

that she served her husband better by being herself than by pretending ways that were not hers. Her compassion and determination helped her husband grow. If a woman thinks she has to adapt to the point of becoming like her husband, if she gives him back only a reflection of himself, she will not be the kind of helper God intended.

Letting Your Husband Be Himself

The tendency in marriage is to try to change each other. Keirsey and Bates in their book *Please Understand Me* say, "It is as if the marriage license is construed as a sculptor's license, giving each spouse the warrant to chisel away until the other becomes the spit and image of the sculptor."[2] Think what irony if both partners succeeded!

We wives want to change our husbands as much as they want to change us. We can get so caught up in what they are not, that we fail to see the good of who they are. One woman fell in love with a man who was a concert pianist. As soon as they set their wedding date, she told him that she expected him to give up his music when they were married. Can you imagine the unhappiness this man would have experienced if he had given in to her desire? But she seemed to think of him as no one, apart from their relationship.

In marriage, we have a special opportunity to see the spark of uniqueness, even genius, in another person. We can criticize and berate and squeeze our husbands into what is, for us, a more comfortable mold. Or we can encourage their uniqueness. When we do this, we give them the chance to discover that for which they were made.

Even flaws in a husband's character can have value. Jeremy Taylor encourages learning to tolerate a spouse's weaknesses. He says we must learn to tolerate our spouse's infirmities, because in doing so we either cure them or make ourselves better.[3]

Manoah's wife could have berated her husband for his impulsiveness. She could have told him he should be content with one appearance of the angel. She could have said that to ask God for more was being presumptuous. But she was respectful and supportive. She let Manoah be himself, and she and her husband were given a day together that they would never forget. The angel of the Lord appeared again, spent hours with them, and even performed miracles.

Working Together

Manoah and his wife had real differences. But their unity was also real. Manoah was bold; his wife was shy. He was a person of action.

12

She was a person who liked to contemplate, to wait and see and think. Manoah needed his wife's otherness. After the angel ascended, it was his wife who filled in the gaps of his understanding and gave him stability. They are a vivid example of unity in diversity.

A modern man and woman who married late in life understood their own individuality and valued each other's uniqueness. The wife was conceptual and creative. The husband was practical and concerned with details. He teased her about her lack of practicality. But he also encouraged her ideas and continually praised her creativity.

She laughed about how they had to decide whether to keep their bank book the way she did, which was to round off all the numbers to the next "10," or to be precise the way he was. "He has the part of the brain I don't have," she says. "I love to let him keep the accounts." Because they accepted each other, she became more productive than ever, and he grew more relaxed and confident.

God created us to be different from our partners so we would blend to make a smooth functioning unit. Our differences are to mesh like interlocking the fingers of your right hand with those of your left.

It isn't easy to learn to live in harmony with a spouse who sees things scientifically when you see everything in terms of relationships. It isn't easy to live with someone who is unemotional when you express emotions freely. It isn't easy to live with a task-oriented spouse if you love to relax and enjoy life. But such differences, discussed and accepted, can be the very strength of a marriage.

For Personal Meditation
"As every man hath received the gift, even so minister the same one to one another, as good stewards of the manifold grace of God."
—1 Peter 4:10, KJV

PATHFINDING WITH YOUR HUSBAND (Important!)

Plan a walk together or an early breakfast out or a dessert alone. Do *one* of the following activities together. Record insights from your discussion.
1. Discuss these quotes:
   "Mutuality takes two whole humans."[4]

"Marriage partners can learn and practice the art of making mental and emotional space—psychic space we might call it—in any situation in which [they] find themselves.... This gives [the other] person room to grow."[5]

2. Compare your personalities and gifts, using the list you have already made in *Exploring Your Uniqueness*. Discuss: How do you try to mold each other into images of yourselves?

3. Read the *Interpreting the Data* section together. Discuss.

LIVING WITH A PASSIVE HUSBAND
A Fresh Look at Headship

LESSONS FROM THE MARRIAGE OF ISAAC AND REBEKAH

Her husband was very ill. She tiptoed in and out of his room, keeping his water cup filled, checking his temperature, making sure he was never alone. She tried to feel soft toward him, but her kindness was all on the outside. She had grown recalcitrant and hard.

He feigned sleep, listening to the clink of her bracelets and imagining the bright colors she wore. How he had loved her when they were young! If only he had known then what he knew now, he would have done things differently. But it was too late, and he was too tired to try anymore.

She was asking a question. Would he like something to eat—some porridge, some cakes? She had made the kind he liked best ... figs that were ripening on the tree in the front yard ... some juice from his favorite vine. He pretended he didn't hear, and she left with an exasperated sigh. She knew him too well.

Married to an Opposite
1. Read Genesis 24:1-61. How would you describe Rebekah's personality? (Note verses 18, 20, 24-25, 28, 55-57.)

Note: *The Hebrew word used to describe Rebekah's beauty* (meod) *means force or intensity.*

Read Genesis 24:62-67. How would you describe Isaac's personality? (For further clues read Genesis 26:18-25.)

Continue reading the rest of Isaac and Rebekah's story in Genesis 25:20-28; Genesis 26:34-35, and Genesis 27:1–28:5. How did Isaac succeed in being a wise and loving leader?

How did he fail?

Describe the progression of his and Rebekah's relationship.

2. Why do you think Rebekah seemed so special to Isaac at first?

David Keirsey and Marilyn Bates in *Please Understand Me* observe that each one of us casts a shadow "of all that one has not developed, expressed, or lived out in oneself . . . and we grope around for that rejected, abandoned, or unlived half of ourselves, like a worm cut in two that goes wriggling around trying to join up with the other end. So the search for our other side is built in, imprinted, . . . and quite imperative."[1]

3. Read the following definitions and choose the phrases that best describe Isaac and Rebekah:

Passive—Offering no opposition or resistance; yielding; patient; taking no active part
Aggressive—full of enterprise and initiative; bold and active; pushing; ready or willing to take issue or engage in direct action; starting quarrels

4. a. How are you like, or not like, Rebekah?

b. How is your husband like, or not like, Isaac?

The Beginnings of Conflict

5. What conflicts did Isaac and Rebekah have? (Genesis 25:24-34)

6. Choose *one* of the following:
- ❧ Write an imaginary scene about some kind of conflict Rebekah might have had with the teenager Esau in the daily events of life. You can make them a modern mother and son or set your scenario in Bible times.
- ❧ Make a list of their possible conflicts.
- ❧ Write out your thoughts on the kind of day-to-day relationship Rebekah may have had with the teenager Jacob.

7. What family tensions surrounding Esau continued into his adulthood? (Genesis 26:34-35)

8. What principles can a wife with a passive husband glean from Christ's parable about prayer in Luke 18:1-8?

9. Rebekah was the one who received the prophecy about God's plan to use Jacob as a leader instead of Esau. In light of Isaac's God-given role as leader of his home, what responsibility did he have concerning his wife's word from God? (Review Genesis 25:21-26.)

Note: *The Bible Knowledge Commentary* says that "Isaac knew of God's oracle to Rebekah . . . that the elder would serve the younger; yet he set out to thwart it by blessing Esau!"[2]

10. What are the major sources of conflict between you and your husband?

How Isaac and Rebekah Failed to Work Together
11. What does Genesis 27:5-13 indicate about the relationship between Isaac and Rebekah?

12. The son who received the patriarchal blessing received the bulk of his father's wealth when he died. He also became the leader of the family. What was right about what Rebekah did?

    What was wrong?

13. If you had been in Rebekah's place, what would you have done differently (or what do you hope that you would have done differently)?

A Godly Headship
14. Read Ephesians 5:23-33 and 1 Peter 3:7. What words here describe a godly husband?

15. List some things your husband does that make you feel led in a loving way.

16. Read the following verses. Star the one that speaks to you about your feelings toward your husband's lack of action.

❦ Colossians 3:12-13
❦ Hebrews 12:15
❦ Proverbs 21:9

EXPLORING YOUR UNIQUENESS

17. Choose *one* of the following for your journal.
❦ Arrange these descriptions into a creative chart.

My husband _____:
         (his name)

Is a fast worker
Makes decisions easily
Puts off making decisions
Is aggressive in some areas,
  not others
Is highly goal-oriented
Likes a head-on argument
Wants problems solved right now
Plans ahead
Always feels everything will
  work out
Is not the idea person in
  our family

Is a slow worker
Takes the lead in groups
Has few goals
Is patient
Is the faith-person in our
  family
Is impatient
Is the worrier in our family
Floats through and enjoys life
Avoids conflict
Listens but often doesn't act

❦ If your husband is not taking action in an area you are concerned about, journal your frustrations and ideas about the issue.
❦ If you feel you need to accept your husband as he is right now and trust God, read Psalm 37:4-6 and Proverbs 3:5-6 and:
  —Copy your favorite phrase. (Illustrate if desired.)
  —List the conflicts for which you will use this verse.

INTERPRETING THE DATA

A Loving Leader

I once read about a man who believed that to be the head of the home meant to have total control. One of the first things he did when he and his wife were married was to make a long list of rules about how he wanted the house kept, the meals cooked, and the laundry done. He demanded that his wife follow all these rules. When she failed, he became angry.

The wife resisted in her heart, but silently endured his demands, doing her best to please him when she could. After they had been married about twenty years, he died.

Later the woman married again. Her second husband did all that he could each day to show her how much he loved her. He listened to her and took immediate action to alleviate anything that frustrated or pained her. He wanted her to be happy. One day the woman discovered, in a drawer, the list that her first husband had given her. She read the rules and was amazed to discover that she was doing all these things for her second husband — even without the list of rules. His love had made all the difference.

When God says that a husband is to be the head of the wife, he means that, first and foremost, a husband is to love his wife. The outworking of this love will be that the husband will lead his wife in thoughtful, understanding ways — protecting her, acting on her insights, and taking the initiative to meet her needs because he considers them as important as his own.

People are, by nature, responders. If a husband listens to his wife, she will listen to him. If he tries to control her, she will try to control him. If he betrays her confidence, as Isaac betrayed Rebekah's by not acting on her revelation from God, his wife may respond in an act of betrayal. If, however, he loves her and seeks to be strong on her behalf, she will respond with love and a desire to serve.

A Quiet Man's Dilemma

A quiet, easy-going man who has a bold wife may feel that his marriage is more of a challenge than he can manage. The *Wycliffe Bible Commentary* describes Isaac and Rebekah's marriage this way: "The man of quiet passive timid faith was joined in marriage to a woman so bold, so adventurous, so ambitious, that she was destined to bring him grief in the years ahead. Yet God was leading, and would use even these imperfect individuals to work out His will for His people."[3]

At the beginning of their marriage, Isaac sensed how much he needed Rebekah's kind of person. We are told that "[Rebekah] became [Isaac's] wife, and he loved her; and Isaac was comforted after his mother's death" (Genesis 24:67). The Hebrew word for comforted (nacham) means to give strength or staying power. Rebekah's zest for life was like cinnamon and sugar stirred into Isaac's oatmeal existence. It was the vitamin he needed to grow eager to live again.

There is also indication that Rebekah realized her need for Isaac's faith and steadiness. He prayed for her and she conceived. He was probably a great encouragement to her during her barren years.

One modern wife who is energetic and aggressive like Rebekah says that she wishes her husband would be the one to initiate ideas for problem-solving. But ideas are not his strength, and she often tires of having to do the "idea-work" in their family.

In spite of this frustration, however, they have a good marriage because the husband leads by loving example. He values her ideas and lives a life of faith. His quiet trust inspires his wife to cultivate patience and tone down the clamoring, jumbled kind of life she would live if left to herself. They need each other.

In his book *The Husband Handbook*, Bob Moorehead says that man is designed to be a strong post on which the female leans.[4]

A "passive husband/aggressive wife" marriage *can* be a good marriage, but it won't be, if the husband fails to realize that sometimes even a strong woman needs to lean on her husband.

During the women's movement that churned to momentum in the 1960's, feminist Merle Shain sought equality with a passion. She worked to gain all the privileges and responsibilities of a man. But in 1989, she wrote a book in which she questioned the validity of these extremes.

In the book *Courage My Love*, Shain tells about how she and a date were discussing the expenses for a special evening out.

" 'Let's just divide them down the middle,' he suggested. 'It's the easiest.'

" 'Even [the meal?' she] whined, feeling unliberated and more than a little silly.

" 'Sure, why not?' he countered. 'What's wrong with that?'

" 'Nothing,' [she] said, 'I guess.' "[5]

But the truth was that his attitude made her feel unloved and insecure. Shain concludes that women have traded protection for equality and are beginning to realize it was not a good bargain.

There are times when every woman needs to feel that she is being protected. A husband can meet this need by something as simple as thinking ahead and buying a space heater for his wife's study because she is more cold-natured than he, or noticing when she is feeling overwhelmed and encouraging her to rest while he does her errands.

One husband, who loves his wife, feels that a good husband should be willing to use money to buy emotional resources for his wife. One time his wife planned to drive 1,000 miles to take their children to see her parents. As the trip drew near, she developed pain in her chest. The doctor said that she was under stress. But the couple couldn't figure out why. Then the husband realized that it might be the long drive, which they were doing just to save money.

He decided to purchase bus tickets for his wife and children, and her chest pain soon left. She felt protected. Their marriage was strengthened. And God was faithful to meet their financial needs.

A Strong Woman's Responsibility

If a husband continues to fail to take action on an important need or issue, it is the wife's responsibility to persevere in discussing the problem with him, with softness and an attitude of respect.

Some will say that if you tell your husband anything more than once you are nagging. But an intense woman who has an easy-going husband will almost always have to say things more than once. As one seminar leader said, such a man needs his wife to be a "Holy Irritant."

A modern woman tells about an instance when she wished she had persevered in sharing a problem with her husband. She and her husband could not agree on how to deal with the lack of respect from their teenage daughters. She thought that when the girls criticized her and said derogatory things about her friends or interests, they were being disrespectful. Her husband didn't agree. The woman had always understood that the most important responsibility of a Christian wife was submission to her husband, and she understood submission to mean that she should share her view once and leave the rest to God. That's what she did.

The girls became more and more discourteous toward her and others. Later their lack of respect for authority caused them to experience difficulty in their careers and marriages. As the years passed, the wife became convinced that a portion of the fault was hers. She felt that she should have persevered in discussing the issue of respect with her husband while the girls were still young.

If a wife continues to share her specific concerns with her husband, and he still doesn't change, if in fact he tells her not to speak of those concerns again, she must weigh the importance of her concerns and the effect on her family if she drops the issue. She must ask herself pointed questions: Is my request selfish? Is it mostly a matter of preference or convenience? Is it a front for a larger issue that my husband and I must deal with in a more forthright way? Is the issue important enough to disrupt our harmony now in order to achieve lasting harmony later? Is my request critical to the well-being of my family? She must pray, follow the teachings of Scripture, and ask God's help for herself, her husband, and her marriage. Then she must act—using the good sense that God has given her.

Most of us have times when we are like Rebekah. We see our husbands set on doing what we know isn't best (though the situation is not life threatening or soul threatening). We try to talk to them, but they refuse to listen. Finally, we become so panicked that we forge ahead with our own driven plans, heedless of the consequences.

It was God's plan to give Jacob the leadership of the family. He certainly could have done that without Rebekah's scheming, and He would have. Rebekah seemed to know very little about faith.

The truth is, however, that it is much easier to talk about faith than it is to practice it. George MacDonald says, "Human nature [never puts] forth such power . . . with such energy as when exercising faith in God. . . . Faith is the highest and sometimes the most difficult work a person can do."[6] We want our children to show strong character *now*. We want our husbands to lead lovingly in *today's* situation, not tomorrow's.

The faith process is like waiting for bread to rise. We get impatient with the time it takes and think it will work just as well to put the bread in the oven an hour early. But if we do, the bread becomes heavy and soggy. We get a mediocre, if not unpalatable, product.

Faith means remembering that it is God's way to give us our heart's desire at the time when the blessings will be the fullest and best. It means reviewing the ways God has been faithful in the past and acting on the belief that He is the same today. God says He will teach our children and give them peace, and He promises the believer a future and a hope (Isaiah 54:13). He is infinitely creative, a God of surprises, who weaves happenings we would never think redeemable into patterns for good.

We can trust such a husband-God with every detail of our lives.

For Personal Meditation
"Trust in the Lord with all your heart and lean not on your own understanding; in all your ways acknowledge Him, and He will make your paths straight."

—Proverbs 3:5-6

PATHFINDING WITH YOUR HUSBAND (Strategic!)

Go to a park for a simple picnic with your husband or light a candle over dessert some evening and choose one of the following activities.
1. Discuss your reactions to the following poem.

The Longing to Be Led

Lead me
But not with hard, immoveable words.
Protect me;
Guide me with wisdom and concern for how I feel.
Then I won't be so alone.

—RAR

2. Read and discuss *Interpreting the Data* together.

EXPLORING YOUR UNIQUENESS (Continued)

❧ Write about your discussion in your journal.
❧ Review the personal meditation quote in this chapter and Lesson 1. Decide how you will use them. Ideas: Memorize them; post them for meditation; write your favorite phrases in calligraphy.

THE TWO WHO BECAME ONE
The Essence of Oneness

LESSONS FROM THE MARRIAGE OF ELIZABETH AND ZECHARIAH

His wife's eyes were red with weeping. He arranged the blankets around her against the cold night air, and she touched his hand. "I think it's time for me to begin confessing my sins."

He sighed. "But there's nothing you need to confess."

"You know it's our custom. And there may be something I've forgotten. I'd like to go to Jerusalem too and offer a sacrifice."

Zechariah felt sad. It was difficult not to hate the women who had slandered his wife in the marketplace that day.

"All right," he said. "If you feel strongly about it, then that's what we'll do."

He caressed Elizabeth's cheek with a light stroke of his finger, knew its familiar softness—no longer young and taut. Together they planned their trip.

The Same Values
1. Read Luke 1:5-25, 39-45, 56-80.

❧ What do we know about Zechariah from Luke 1:5-7?

❧ Elizabeth?

The priests who served in the temple were all descendants of Aaron. They were divided into twenty-four classes. The class of Abijah was one of the most highly respected. Each class officiated in turn at the temple in Jerusalem for one week at a time. The weeks they weren't serving, they lived in other cities, often working as teachers in their local synagogues.[1]

2. The Greek word for righteous (or upright) is *dikaios*. It can also be translated *correct* or *innocent*. What light does Philippians 2:14-15 shed on the way an "upright" person lives from day-to-day?

3. Check the words that best describe this couple's relationship:
   –unequal   –healthy
   –conflict-oriented   –built around the same values
   –characterized by mutual respect   –supportive
   –disappointing   –bitter

4. Write out a few thoughts about what you understand oneness to mean in marriage.

Elizabeth's Needs

5. What special need did Elizabeth have? (Luke 1:7, 25)

Note: *In Elizabeth's time, people believed infertility was a result of some major disobedience, a chastisement from the Lord.* The Bible Almanac says, "*It is hard for us to imagine how devastating these events would have been for the childless wife. She was spiritually ruined, socially disgraced, and psychologically depressed.*"[2]

6. Elizabeth had come to be called the Barren One (verse 36). For some, this designation probably began as a ridicule. How do you think Zechariah responded when his peers (some of them scribes and Pharisees) slandered Elizabeth? Consider Luke 1:6 and Matthew 23:23.

Note: *Zechariah did not live by the letter of the law alone. He would understand the heart of the Hebrew teaching about the home: that the husband was to "lovingly [assume] responsibility for the family and . . . serve the needs of those who were under his authority . . . [that] the wife was to help her husband, [but] the husband was [also] to care for his wife."*[3]

7. What is one of your needs right now? How does your husband make you feel that he is one with you (or not one with you) in this area?

8. How would God like to meet your needs even if your husband doesn't?

   ❦ Isaiah 41:10

   ❦ Hosea 11:4

Zechariah's Needs

9. Record any hints you see in the following verses about Zechariah's personality and needs (Luke 1:12-23, 64).

10. The wives of the priests often accompanied them to the temple, but Elizabeth was not with Zechariah at this time. How do you think he felt about being alone during this eventful week? Choose one of the following activities for fleshing out your answer:

    ❦ Write a monologue or a poem describing Zechariah's thoughts about Elizabeth during the events in the temple.

❦ Finish the following sentence: "If I were Zechariah and knew that I had to finish several more days at the temple without being able to speak, I would . . . !

11. What clues do the following verses give us about the way Elizabeth related to her husband after his return from the temple? (Luke 1:23-24, 45, 59-64)

12. Write about a time that you supported your husband when he was confused or discouraged. Or write about a time when you wished that you had supported him.

Mutual Support—What We Can Do

13. Mutual support is an important goal in marriage, but we need to begin by concentrating on our part. Every man is unique. Some men have difficulty admitting their needs. Wives of these men will find it difficult to think of ways to give them emotional support. If this is true of your husband, you can begin addressing your dilemma by being willing to do things that you know please him. Mark the items below that your husband especially likes you to do.
   – Listen while he shares about problems at work
   – Cook attractive meals on a regular basis
   – Budget wisely
   – Do projects with him
   – Plan fun activities to do together
   – Other _____
   What could you do this week in one of these areas?

If you feel your husband demands too much in some area, what compromise could you discuss with him?

EXPLORING YOUR UNIQUENESS

14. Choose *one* of the following exercises:
    - ❦ Draw a picture or a diagram that illustrates an area where you and your husband disagree. Then draw another one that shows the way you would like it to be.
    - ❦ Record a recent experience in your marriage that demonstrates some kind of oneness. Then write a prayer or a poem thanking God for that progress in your marriage.
    - ❦ If your husband is not supporting you in an area of need (or if you are not supporting him), do some brainstorming with a trusted friend about how to begin solving that problem. Or fill a journal page with ideas.

INTERPRETING THE DATA

The husband was sitting at the café breakfast bar. His wife came in from shopping and gave him a hug. The waitress watched the old couple greedily, longing for what they had.

They discussed the menu in whispers. When the waitress asked them for their order, he started a sentence and his wife softly finished it. Then they both nodded.

The girl who was waiting on Mr. and Mrs. Dillard had known them for a long time. They attended the same church. The Dillards had been missionaries in Indonesia for thirty years, and even here in the States they still had their causes. He walked marathons to raise money for charity, and she did the paperwork and made the calls. She led women's Bible studies. He prayed with her before the women came. They prepared the house together. After the waitress had brought them their muffins and juice, they said a quiet blessing and then smiled at each other.

Even though the young waitress had been married several years, she and her husband had conflicts they couldn't seem to resolve. As she cleared off the other end of the counter, she beat the air with her silent prayers. "How, Lord, is such oneness achieved? Did You mean only physical oneness when You said with such sureness, 'The two shall become one flesh,' or do You really have in mind totality—spiritual, emotional, and mental, as well as physical? Is such oneness possible only if two people have temperaments and backgrounds that are the same? Or can it be cultivated and won? Is there hope for me—and my husband? What did you mean for me, Lord, when You said, 'The two shall become one'?" (See Matthew 19:3-6.)

There are many misconceptions in the Christian culture today about marital oneness. Before we can begin any effective work on oneness in our marriages, it is essential that we understand the true definition of oneness.

What Oneness Isn't

Some teach that if a husband and wife are deeply spiritual, the husband will dominate, and the wife will become silent. It is said that then and only then will oneness be total. There will be one personality, and it will be the husband's.

Other couples achieve a similar oneness by the wife dominating and the husband becoming silent. Again, there is one personality, but this time it is the wife's.

How could either scenario be what is best for the silent partner? This is a pretend kind of oneness, a oneness in which a unique individual is obliterated in order to keep the peace.

Another common definition of oneness is never being apart. Marriage counselors Howard and Charlotte Clinebell warn couples about the dangers of this misconception. "It is a costly fallacy to assume ... that an 'intimate marriage' is one in which husband and wife does everything together. ... One of the marks of genuine intimacy is the respect for the need of each partner for periods of aloneness—for the natural rhythm of solitude and intimacy."[4]

Some people need more time alone than others in order to cope with life. If a wife is a people person and a husband likes to study and think, and the wife refuses to give him the space he needs, he will feel unloved. She will undermine their oneness.

Lois Wyse speaks to this issue in her *Love Poems for the Very Married:*

Intimacy and Autonomy

There is within each of us
A private place
For thinking private thoughts
And dreaming private dreams.

But in the shared experience of marriage,
Some people cannot stand the private partner.
How fortunate for me
That you have let me grow,
Think my private thoughts,
Dream my private dreams.

And bring a private me
To the shared experience of marriage.

—*Lois Wyse*[5]

Another common definition of oneness is sameness. If you are a great deal alike, if you have similar backgrounds the way Elizabeth and Zechariah did, it will be easier to attain a high degree of oneness. In our culture, however, we often marry opposites. As we've already seen, in the study on Manoah, differences can be the strength of a marriage, contributing to a powerful teamwork.

Defining Oneness

My husband and I know a couple who are different from each other in many ways, but there is an aura of oneness about their marriage that you can't miss. When we asked the husband how he would define oneness, he said, "I think of it as mutual support, as wanting 100 percent what is best for your spouse." There was something more true in this husband's definition than any other I'd heard.

Another man, who has a happy marriage, enlarges this definition when he tells about his and his wife's experience. "When I first got married," he said, "I felt I had to have the last say, no matter what. I guess I thought that was what being a strong husband was. Then I noticed that my wife began to be afraid to share her feelings with me and became very unhappy. Something was wrong. I wanted her to be happy. If I was the cause of her unhappiness, it must be that the macho image I'd thought was right really wasn't.

31

"I began encouraging her to be open with me. I learned to think of her feelings, her frustrations, and her yearnings as mine. When she was sad, I wanted to get involved, because we were one. Part of me became sad. I had to do something to help her."

In a marriage where there is genuine oneness, the joy of one is the joy of the other, the unhappiness of one is the unhappiness of the other. Each partner, therefore, becomes a key resource to the other.

How We Can Support Each Other

In Elizabeth and Zechariah's time, childlessness was a major threat to a marriage. Husbands often divorced barren wives in order to marry someone who could give them a child. Or if the husband didn't demand a divorce, he grew so resentful that he made life unbearable for his wife.

The oneness of Elizabeth and Zechariah tints each portion of the picture Scripture shows of their lives. Zechariah would have been the kind of husband who would consider any ridicule Elizabeth experienced as his own. He would have comforted her and believed in her through it all.

And Elizabeth was the kind of wife who would have welcomed her wounded husband home after his encounter with the angel, prepared his favorite meal, and encouraged him through his sense of failure.

What makes a husband or wife feel supported varies from one marriage to another—because every marriage is different. One husband says he feels supported by his wife when she communicates that she is available to him and lets him know she values his ideas. Another husband says the fact that his wife is considerate of his need for spontaneity and freedom gives him a sense of support.

Wives too experience support in a variety of ways. My husband has a practical bent, so I've learned that the easiest way for him to support me is through practical activity. I feel supported when he listens to my dreams and takes practical steps to bring them to pass. But a friend says that her husband communicates support to her when he helps her clean house and remembers their traditions on anniversaries.

One night a man came home exhausted—feeling that he had no resources to give to anyone. He tried to hide his bad mood, but did not succeed. After supper he decided to slip upstairs and go to bed early.

After he had been in bed for about fifteen minutes, he heard his wife open the bedroom door. He groaned, kept his eyes shut, and prayed, "Lord, I love this woman, but please make her go away!" Then he heard the door close—slowly, quietly.

The next morning when his wife asked him how he was, he thanked her for supporting him by letting him be alone and rest.

Mutual support is showing that we want 100 percent what is best for our spouse. It means being alert to their desires, hurts, and moods. It means doing our best to help and encourage. Sometimes mutual support means listening; at other times it means getting involved in a practical way. But it always means being sensitive and willing to serve the other person right where he (or she) is. This is the essence of oneness.

For Personal Meditation:
"... make my joy complete by being like-minded, having the same love, being one in spirit and purpose. . . . Each of you should look not only to your own interests, but also to the interests of others."
—Philippians 2:2, 4

PATHFINDING WITH YOUR HUSBAND

Put on a CD of old favorites or play a favorite game from your past. Then take twenty minutes to do one of the activities below:
❦ Without discussion, each of you write your own answer to this question: What is oneness? Write for five minutes, then share the results.
❦ Read and discuss the *Interpreting Your Data* section.

EXPLORING YOUR UNIQUENESS (Continued)

Journal about your discussion.

4

SURVIVING A DIFFICULT MARRIAGE
The Importance of Listening to Your Spouse

LESSONS FROM THE MARRIAGE OF ABIGAIL AND NABAL

She woke feeling free. Her husband was gone, attending to business in Carmel. Today she could lose herself in creative household affairs without the weight of his constant displeasure. She dressed for the day and hurried to the kitchen. Her servants had already begun making the cheese. She checked their progress and then began measuring spices for the cakes they would need for the shearing festival.

As she worked, she thought about how David's band of men had helped guard their flocks during the year. Some said David would be the next king. . . . And her husband was ignoring him! Nothing she could say would make any difference. Nabal always laughed at her when she questioned him about how he handled his business. He told her she knew nothing about such matters. Finally she quit trying to reason with him about anything. He went his way, and she went hers.

Nabal and Abigail's Personalities
1. Read 1 Samuel 25:1-39.
   a. Describe the main characters in this story.

   b. What recurrent theme do you see in verses 17, 24, 35-36?

2. Match the following phrases. (Have fun with your lines: draw loops, waves, rickrack, etc.)

Nabal was	intelligent
Abigail was	worthless
Nabal	possessed many riches
Abigail said	had returned evil for good
David felt Nabal	folly is with him
Nabal became	listened
Nabal	spoke words from God
David felt Abigail	was beautiful
Abigail	very drunk
David	did not listen

Note: *Abigail's name means "cause of joy," and yet there is no indication Nabal valued her at all.*

3. David was hiding from King Saul's wrath in the caves and hills of the Judean wilderness. He had a following of six hundred men. Instead of preying on Nabal's flocks to provide for their food, David's men helped protect Nabal's flocks from wild beasts and robbers. It is still the custom among roving tribes in this part of the world to levy protection money. "In return for gifts, they guarantee the protection of life and property in these notoriously insecure districts."[1]

❦ Compare the spirit of David's plea to Nabal's answer in 1 Samuel 25:4-11.

❦ What revealing words recur more than once in verse 11?

❦ The meaning of the name Nabal is *fool*. In what ways did Nabal live up to his name?

The Marriage's Personality

4. What does 1 Samuel 25:19 tell us about Nabal and Abigail's relationship?

1 Samuel 25:23-25?

5. Choose *one* of the following creative exercises to depict the kind of conversation Abigail and Nabal may have had in the early days of their marriage.

❦ Choose and illustrate a descriptive word or phrase.
❦ Draw a cartoon strip with four frames.
❦ Write a paragraph from Abigail's point of view.

6. What were God's reasons for instituting marriage? (Genesis 2:18)

Does the fact that you are married mean that you never feel alone? Explain your answer.

7. Think of a time when your husband truly listened to you. What did it do for your relationship?

8. How can the truths in Psalm 62:8 help you if your husband is not a good listener?

Henry Nouwen says, "God wants to offer us a solid love to dwell in, a firm ground to stand on, a faithful presence to trust in."² If Abigail had looked at her marriage from a human standpoint, she would have grown bitter and revengeful. Instead, she learned when to be quiet and when to act and grow beautiful inside, as well as out.

Genuine Listening and Its Benefits

9. How might things have been different in Nabal's life if he had cultivated the habit of listening to Abigail the way David did?

10. Look up the following words in a dictionary and record your favorite definition for each.

   Listen

   Dialogue

11. What qualities does a person need in his or her life in order to be able to fully listen to others?

   Walter Wangerin in *As for Me and My House* writes, "King Solomon asked for 'an understanding heart,' also translated a 'hearing heart.' The genius of wisdom . . . is the ability to open a room in one's heart for the talk — and so for the presence — of another."[3]

12. There is a little of Nabal's inability to listen in all of us. If you ever have difficulty being genuinely open to your husband's thoughts, place your initials in front of the statements that best describe the reasons for your difficulty.

❦ Our values are too different to communicate on certain subjects.
❦ I feel I'm right.
❦ I'm more worried about my needs than his.
❦ I don't feel my husband has anything to contribute to my life.
❦ I know what he will say (or not say).
❦ I'm not interested in the same things he is.
❦ Other _____.

EXPLORING YOUR UNIQUENESS

13. Choose *one* activity for your journal:
    ❦ If you have a difficult marriage and feel that you are growing bitter, write honestly about your feelings. Then study Ephesians 4:29-32. Conclude with a prayer that reflects your response to that passage.
    ❦ If you want to work at being a better listener, read Proverbs 18:13 and Proverbs 19:20. Paraphrase the verse you like best. Reflect on how you would like to apply this verse to your life this week.
    ❦ Write a limerick about reasons you and your husband have difficulty dialoguing. Use the following form:

    When we fuss and we cry and we fume,
    "Give me this; give me that; I want room!"
    And don't feel the breeze
    Or see the green trees,
    We build custom castles of gloom.

INTERPRETING THE DATA

The Importance of Mutual Listening
In their book *The Intimate Marriage*, Howard and Charlotte Clinebell say, "In some marriages the 'we' feeling never develops . . . [the couple] live alone together as though they were still single psychologically."[4]

Abigail and Nabal had this type of marriage. It was difficult for them to even want to listen to one another. Their values were at opposite extremes.

Perhaps Abigail despaired:

We talk; we try,
But the river between us is too wide.
You cannot hear;
I am alone.
You walk, eyes riveted to the track,
And I have learned to be silent.
My singing hurts your ears.
Each day I wait.
And when you need my service no more,
I fly free and sing and think and pray:
For a moment, no longer alone.

—RAR

Loneliness is part of the human condition, always with us until death, but marriage can lessen its intensity if both spouses truly listen to one another. Without good dialogue, a marriage dies. The partners live alone.

In his book, *The Miracle of Dialogue*, Reuel L. Howe defines dialogue as "the serious address and response between two or more persons, in which the being and truth of each is confronted by the being and truth of the other."[5]

Hindrances to Dialogue

When a wife talks nonstop, so focused on her own needs that she has no room for her husband's needs, she hinders dialogue. Her actions say, "I am not interested in the 'being and truth' of you."

Another hindrance to good dialogue is pride. Once, in a Bible study discussion, I asked a group of women if they would tell about a time when they wished they had been more open to their husbands' ideas. One of them responded immediately. "I can't think of a single time," she said. "I'm always right." She laughed, and we all laughed with her—probably because each of us often felt the same way. We just weren't bold enough to admit it.

But if we are convinced that we are always right, our spouses will sense that attitude. Our pride will make it hard for them to speak freely, even when we try to listen.

Another hindrance to dialogue is assuming that we know everything our spouse is going to say about the subject before we discuss it. Walter Wangerin observes, "[Even in marriage] you never completely know the other. And the assumption that you do only hinders your true listening and so keeps you from knowing him or her. . . . One of the most common and desperate maladies of marriage [is] to imprison the spouse in our own image of the spouse."[6]

Sometimes husbands have an attitude that keeps wives from speaking freely, an attitude we might call "the Tartar viewpoint" of marriage. The Tartar in Maxim Gorkie's play *The Lower Depth* expresses his view toward marriage this way, "Ugh, mad folks these Russian women! Hussies, unmanageable. The Tartar women are not so; they know the law."[7]

The "Tartar" type of husband wants the husband-wife relationship to be like that of lord and serf, when God meant it to be a relationship of protector and completer.

One husband who understands dialogue in a Christian marriage says, "I believe my wife has just as much access to the Spirit of God as I do. I listen carefully, especially when she disagrees with me. I know that the Lord may be speaking through her. I can't be too proud to listen to what she has to say."

Every man feels frustrated when his wife disagrees with him. Some men feel that they have failed. But both husband and wife need to understand that it is okay for a wife to disagree. The man demonstrates acceptance of the woman's personhood when he listens and refuses to become defensive. The woman helps her husband grow and often strengthens him when she speaks her disagreement with a gentle honesty.

Abigail accepted the truth about who Nabal was and what was lacking in their relationship. She didn't overspiritualize and pretend her situation was something it was not. Some Christians have criticized her for showing her disagreement with her husband by taking provisions to David. But God honored Abigail's actions, and by those actions, she saved her husband's life—albeit temporarily. One commentary explains, ". . . [Because Abigail perceived] Nabal's stubbornness would ruin them all, the [urgency] of the situation fully justified her conduct. . . . Inferior interests must always be sacrificed to secure the greater."[8]

Learning to Dialogue

Every marriage has its limits. Striving to make our marriage like someone else's can hinder instead of help. It can keep us from achieving the best that is possible in our situation. Even in a good marriage, there are times when love seems to be over. Accepting these facts can help us focus on forging a workable relationship, rather than the impossibility of a perfect one.

If Nabal had been willing to dialogue with Abigail from the beginning, if he had let her share her being and her truth with him, they may have had a workable marriage. It may never have been ideal, but if there is dialogue, there is always hope. Howe says, "Dialogue can bring into being once again a relationship that has died . . . [but] it must be mutual and proceed from both sides, and the parties to it must persist relentlessly."[9]

Such persistent confronting each other with our being and truth will often involve conflict and hurt that is difficult to endure. In an age when marriage lasts "as long as we both shall love," it is more attractive to run than to stand and do battle for our marriages. We do well to remember the Puritan prayer: "Every new duty calls for more grace than I now possess, but not more than is found in Thee, the divine Treasury."[10]

In *As for Me and My House,* Walter Wangerin tells about how he fell into the habit of putting his parishioners above his family. Without realizing what he was doing, he began to belittle his wife in the presence of others and to make decisions for her as though she were a child. His wife smoldered in silence. She wanted him to notice her needs without her saying anything. She even felt selfish for feeling that way.

Then the day arrived when her loneliness was so intense that she had no strength to pretend any longer. Her bitterness exploded. She confessed her wretchedness to her husband and said she couldn't keep up the farce of being a loving pastor's wife any longer. In the weeks that followed they experienced stark and difficult times.

But in spite of the dark days, this wife's honest confession was the beginning of healing in their marriage. Her husband began to hear her. He discovered that his wife was a person who had her own dreams. He encouraged her and helped her pursue those dreams. And she learned to forgive him and to love him again.

How we wives want our husbands to listen to us in these ways! And they need us to listen to them in the same ways. They need us to pay attention when they want to talk about their interests. They also need us to be sensitive enough and courageous enough to draw them out when they are hurt or confused and even when they are angry. We need to hear, or we will not know. A good listener encourages the other to be himself. She lets him talk into her listening silence; she refuses to insert observation or criticisms. She gives him freedom to reveal his whole being and truth.

The wife who does this for her husband becomes for him a reflection of God, who wants us to pour out our hearts before Him and find in Him a refuge.

The same is true for the husband who does this for his wife.

The Yes

He saw she was hurting, and he didn't know why.
"Talk to me," he said.
"I'm afraid."
"That's why you must talk, to take away your fear."
"You would be angry."
"How can you know?"
"I know what you will say."
"I will not say anything. I will listen."
"There is not time. You have much to do."
"I have all the time you need. The most important thing now
is listening to you."
"And you will hear?"
"I will truly hear."
"And you will not reject me, whoever you see I am?"
"I will love you more because you have opened yourself to me."
She shared, fearful, then growing bold, telling her husband
things she had never shared with anyone.
He drew her words into himself. With his eyes and thought
and loving silence, he prized her otherness.
And she no longer felt alone.

—RAR

For Personal Meditation:
"I love the Lord, because He hears my voice and my supplications."
—Psalm 116:1, NASB

PATHFINDING WITH YOUR HUSBAND
(Life-Changing!)

Go to a favorite spot and discuss *one* of the following:

1. Which words or phrases do you feel best describe a good listener: humble, distracted, emptying ourselves of opinion, affirming, making judgment, commenting, anxious to share your view, focused, encouraging logical thinking, valuing a person's feelings, available only at convenient times, giving answers, quiet, trying to understand, attending closely, casual, disinterested, reacting.

2. "Man is the sole living creature known to us [who] needs confirmation. . . . Again and again the Yes must be spoken to him, from the look of the confidant and from the stirrings of his own heart, to liberate him from the dread of abandonment, which is a foretaste of death."[11]

3. Read and talk about the *Interpreting the Data* Section.

LONGING FOR LOVE
Love's Joys and Limitations

LESSONS FROM THE MARRIAGES OF RACHEL AND JACOB AND HANNAH AND ELKANAH

He had just come in from the fields. It had been a hard day, but the moment he stepped inside the door he felt better.

His wife was sitting on a cushion arranging the dishes for the evening meal. In the center of the low table stood an earthenware pot filled with red and yellow wildflowers. The table was perfect.

Rachel had had a difficult day also. But when her husband took off his cloak, her heart skipped a beat at the sight of his bare arms and the splendid chest that filled the tunic she had made for him. Jacob smiled at his beautiful wife. What surprise did his unpredictable Rachel have for him tonight? A new fragrance, a story to make him laugh, a song on her shepherd's flute? He bent down and gave her a long kiss.

Rachel responded to his kiss with a fierce passion. But Jacob felt her tears on his cheek.

"What's the matter?" he asked.

"I'm sick with envy, Jacob. You must give me a child or I'll die." The flood of words that followed were demanding and incoherent.

Jacob couldn't believe what he was hearing. How could Rachel blame him for her barrenness when he had already produced four children by Leah? The last thing he needed tonight was to have to deal with an irrational woman. His face turned livid with anger.

"You demand too much from me," he said. "As much as I love you, I can't be everything to you, Rachel. No man could."

He jerked on his cloak and left.

Rachel felt whipped. Jacob had never talked to her that way. Did she expect too much of their love?

Surveying the Marriages of Rachel and Hannah
1. Read Genesis 29:1–30:24.

Describe Rachel and Jacob. (Use your imagination to fill in the gaps. *Optional: Refer to Genesis 28:10-22 for more about Jacob.*)

Describe the nature of their relationship.

2. Read 1 Samuel 1:1–2:2
   How do you envision Elkanah?

What was Hannah like?

Hannah's name means "grace or compassion." Describe Hannah and Elkanah's relationship.

Growing in Love
3. Underline the definitions of love you like best:
   ❦ A deep and tender feeling of affection for or attachment to
   ❦ Devotion
   ❦ A strong, passionate affection of one person for another, based in part on sexual attraction
   ❦ Benevolent concern
   ❦ To delight in, take pleasure in
   ❦ "The experience of knowing that another person cares—deeply, warmly, acceptingly, and dependably."[1]

4. Consider what Genesis 31:36, 38-41 tells us about what it was like

to work for Laban. Then paraphrase (expand on) Jacob's love for Rachel as expressed in Genesis 29:20.

5. Review Genesis 29:23-30. Write a paragraph or a poem about how Rachel and Jacob must have felt the first time they made love. (*Optional: Refer to Song of Solomon 1:9-17; 4:9-16 for inspiration.*)

6. Review 1 Samuel 1:5-8, 21-23.
   a. The word *double* in verse 5 is the Hebrew word for anger. This verse could be translated, "But to Hannah he gave an *angry* portion, for he loved Hannah."
   b. A more accurate translation of 1 Samuel 1:23 is "The Lord confirm *thy* word" (meaning Hannah's word).[2]
   c. There is no hint of arrogance in Elkanah when he asks his wife, "Am I not better to you than ten sons?" He was probably a source of cheer and insight—a man much loved by his barren wife.

   What further insights do these facts give you about the kind of love Elkanah had for Hannah?

7. How would you describe your feelings for your husband?

8. Romance may not last forever in a marriage, but we can pray for affection toward our husbands and a growing experience of friendship. Stop now and spend time in prayer. Talk to God about your feelings for your husband—and his feelings for you. Ask your loving Lord to mold those feelings into what is good and to create from them a lasting marriage.

Realizing We Need More
9. The Hebrew word used for Jacob's love for Rachel is *aheb*. It means "to breathe after, to long for, to desire." It is a word that is

often used in a positive sense in Scripture, but sometimes it is used "in a bad sense [describing a] paramour or debauchee." [Then it] contains the idea of idolater. Love, somewhat as fire or water, can be a great blessing and also become a great curse."³

What was wrong with Rachel's attitude in Genesis 30:1-2?

10. Inordinate expectation can damage a relationship. When have you (or your husband) expected too much of your love? What happened?

11. Study more carefully 1 Samuel 1:6-11, 15-16. List all the words that refer to some kind of deep hurt or emotion.

12. Why was Elkanah's love not enough for Hannah? Draw a flower or a star (or something else) next to the best answer.
    She needed to experience God's love.
    Having a child was more important to her than being a good wife.
    Not having a child was an unbearable stigma.
    She was an ungrateful person.

13. Considering the expectations we often have of marriage, what is the significance of Hannah's praise in 1 Samuel 2:2?

EXPLORING YOUR UNIQUENESS

14. In your journal copy Paul's prayer in Ephesians 3:14-21. Substitute the word "I" or "my" for "you."

Keeping in mind the breadth, length, height, and depth of God's love for you, take your longings to Him in *one* of the following ways:

❦ Make a list of your worries and longings. Then pray through your list.

❦ Write a prayer in which you cast all your cares on God the way Hannah did and ask Him to show you His love in a specific area.

❦ Draw or paste pictures in your journal that illustrate some of your main longings. Then pray about them until you feel more at peace.

INTERPRETING THE DATA

The Wonder of Romantic Love

Love is born fair
And full of dreams
And placed unbidden in my hands
I start and gasp.

Was this bare soul mine?
It colors, and I laugh.
At last I can trust; I can lean.

— RAR

One can imagine Rachel thinking these kinds of "falling in love thoughts" during her first month of getting to know Jacob. And Jacob probably walked through the next seven years in a dream-state, living for the times he would see Rachel at meals, or waiting for a chance to help her tend a wounded sheep, or to search for one that was lost. His love for Rachel was so great that the years of grueling labor her father required in return for her hand seemed nothing. For Jacob, his labor was a labor of love. Such motivation and ability to endure is characteristic of the enigma we call romantic love. Against all reason, this love will give up everything to be with the beloved.

A husband desires his wife not only for the pleasure she can give, but also for who she is. Sex becomes a beautiful act in which the husband and wife intentionally give and receive pleasure. "Like a lily among thorns is my darling among the maidens," says the writer of *The Song of Solomon*. "Like an apple tree among the trees of the forest is my lover among the young men. I delight to sit in his shade, and his fruit is sweet to my taste" (Song of Solomon 2:2-3). This love is full of joy, play and a sense of destiny. Some would say romantic love is the only thing worth living for.

Almost every woman longs to be loved with a great love by a man whom she loves the same way. But even if a woman receives this wish she will still experience doubts and moments of emptiness. We all have vast needs, and no human love is complete enough to fill that vastness.

Romantic love is not enough. Friendship is not enough. Even family love is not enough. Only God's love can still the ache for a love that meets our needs: the need to feel beautiful and worthwhile, the need for help, for a steadiness we can count on, the need for direction, for health, for hope.

The Dangers of Turning Love into a God

In his book *The Four Loves*, C.S. Lewis exalts the fulfillment and gladness and comfortableness found in human love. But he returns again and again to the unavoidable premise that if we let any human love rule our lives, it will destroy us.

Leo Tolstoy, in his novel *Anna Karenina*, tells how Anna deserts her husband and gives up her reputation for her lover. As the years pass, her high-flung romance turns parasitic, riddled with suspicion, resentment, and fear. In the end Anna commits suicide.

Rachel's and Leah's "desire for affectionate approval [led them] down dangerous paths."[4] Each woman forced her handmaid on Jacob as an extra wife thinking that if he had more children in her name he would love her more. Poor Jacob! He never wanted any wife except Rachel.

C.S. Lewis tells about a woman who "lived for her family." She did all the laundry, even though they could afford to send it out. She prepared two hot meals for her husband and children every day, even though they asked her not to. She made dresses and knitted countless sweaters that they felt they had to wear. She nursed them herself when they were sick, and when they had activities in the evenings, she waited up for them. She often said she "would 'work her fingers to the bone' for her family. They couldn't stop her."[5]

The sad end to this tale is that the whole family was relieved when she died. At last they could buy the kinds of clothes they liked best, eat out when they wanted, and stay out late.

Human Love Is Not Enough

No matter what godlike qualities are present in the way we love, we are *not* gods. Therefore, any human love will always prove inadequate.

Even if a man loves his wife with an unselfish, sensitive love, she will still have times when she feels that his love is not enough. There may be magic moments when she senses that he sees all the good in her, as well as all the hurt and the flaws — and loves her anyway. He may show that he loves and accepts her by softly touching each part of her: intellectual, emotional, physical, and spiritual. When this happens she gladly yields to him.

This is the kind of love a woman is made for. *But God is the only one who loves this way at all times.* Any man's love will be limited by time and space and his own needs. The most he can do is give his wife glimpses of God's love, samples in tiny packages.

Hannah's husband Elkanah loved her well. His love included tenderness and respect, as well as the fiber of wise leadership. But it still wasn't enough. Hannah needed the concrete experience of God's love.

In one of the most fervent prayers in the Bible, Paul asks God to help believers run after and catch God's love. The *Amplified Bible* uses the word *apprehend* which means to "capture, seize, or take hold of." He prays that each of us may "know — practically, through experience for yourselves — the love of Christ which far surpasses mere knowledge . . . that you may be filled (through all your being) unto all the fullness of God" (Ephesians 3:19, AMP).

Experiencing God's Love

It all sounds so good. But how do we actually experience God's love each day? Four ways emerge: being alert to what He is doing for us today, recognizing His compensations, cultivating a sense of community among believers, and asking God to do a new thing.

Let's enlarge on each of these:

(1) God's love becomes more concrete to us when we review the positives in a day and realize that they came from Him: the rainbow we walk into on a rainy afternoon, the beauty of new snow, some small event that makes us laugh, a good book we "happen" to find on a shelf. "Every good and perfect gift is from above" (James 1:17a).

(2) Everyone has problems. But the psalmist exhorted himself to, "Praise the Lord, O my soul, and forget not all His benefits." (The word translated *benefits* in the NIV is the Hebrew word *gemul*. It can also be translated *recompenses* or *compensations*.) The writer of Jacob's story emphasizes the fact that God loved the unwanted wife Leah and gave her rich compensations in the midst of her oppression. "When the Lord saw that Leah was not loved, He opened her womb" (Genesis 29:31). Leah had six sons of her own and two by her handmaid. Walvoord's *Bible Knowledge Commentary* says, "God chose the despised mother, Leah, and exalted her to be the first mother. The kingly tribe of Judah and the priestly tribe of Levi trace back to her. . . ."[6]

What are your compensations? Reflect on these—and praise God.

(3) God's plan has always been to use the church as community: the hands, the feet, the ears, the eyes working together to meet the needs of each Christian. We are more like pieces of Swiss cheese than steel or granite. No one person (not even a husband) has the resources to fill all the holes in our lives. We need to benefit from the gifts and skills of fellow-believers who make up the full body of Christ.

As I write this, I think of all the ways my Christian friends have helped me "capture" God's love in the last few days. One friend who has a nursing background told me some facts about pain that enabled me to deal more effectively with a medical problem. Another helped me be more content with my limitations when she prayed for me in our Bible study group and asked God to give me "peace within my borders." Another friend called me on Sunday and told me I *must* be at church in time for the third service prelude. When I got there, a string quartet was playing one of my favorite pieces of chamber music. My friends shared from their unique talents and resources. Through them I experienced more of the broadness of God's love.

(4) There are times when God gives us a "divine discontent" because He wants us to pray for change. Hannah prayed out of her agony, and God answered her prayer by creating something new. She cast all of her cares on Him—pouring out every emotion, every need, every desperation—until she reached a point of peace, until she knew that God was going to do something about her situation. What new persons, new factors, new dimensions would God add to our lives if we multiplied our prayers the way Hannah did?

Sometimes God wants us to find healing in acceptance of our situation the way it is: accept the amount and kind of love our husbands can give us or that we can give them; accept the particular struggle God has allowed in our marriages and learn to endure.

At other times, however, God uses discontent like Hannah's. If we are racked with sorrow, as she was, something must be done. Either way, being rooted in God's unconditional love, instead of depending on our spouses alone, will ease our pain.

> *Do husbands fail as part of mighty plan of Yours—*
> *To help us see the pattern, then the breaking,*
> *The hope, the tears, the frantic idol-making,*
> *And learn that You alone are faithful, always there?*
> *God-husband, may I love You best*
> *And find my longed-for place of rest.*
>
> —RAR

For Personal Meditation:
"I led them with cords of a man, with bonds of love, and I became to them as one who lifts the yoke from their jaws; and I bent down and fed them."

—Hosea 11:4 NASB

PATHFINDING WITH YOUR HUSBAND
(Don't Forget!)

Plan breakfast out this Saturday and choose *one* of the activities below:

1. Discuss these quotes and relate them to incidents in your marriage.

   ❦ "Selfish love often appears to be unselfish, because it is willing to make any concession to the beloved in order to keep him prisoner . . . a love . . . that is selfless, that honestly seeks the truth, does not make unlimited concessions to the beloved."[7]

   ❦ What does it mean in everyday terms to "transcend the possessive step in love"?[8]

2. On separate sheets, write things that make you feel loved. Then list what you think makes your spouse feel loved. Discuss.

3. Read the *Interpreting the Data* Section together and discuss.

KNOWING WHEN TO TAKE A STAND
A Balanced Look at Submission

LESSONS FROM THE MARRIAGE OF ESTHER AND XERXES

Her husband chose one of the goblets from a servant's tray and took a sip. He smiled. "My favorite wine. You have been busy today, my dear. This meal is perfect."

She tried to return his smile, but her eyes filled with tears.

He saw and leaned toward her. "What is it? Please tell me what I can do to help."

She shook her head. "Later, perhaps. But I *would* like you to come to dinner again tomorrow night if you can—and bring Haman."

The king's first thought was that Esther was being disobedient not to tell him what she wanted right then. But she seemed so thoughtful of him, so evidently seeking to serve him. He let it go. Esther had always proved worthy of his trust.

The next night when the king asked Esther how he could help, she answered him in a firm, quiet voice. "If I have found favor in your sight, O king, grant me my life and the life of my people, for we have been sold to be annihilated."

When the king asked who it was that had done such a thing, Esther's voice rose and she pointed toward the man sitting across the table. "A foe and an enemy is this wicked man Haman," she said.

Esther had accused her husband's closest adviser and friend, and her husband listened. Haman was hanged within the hour.

The Marriage
1. Read chapters 1–7 of Esther in one sitting.
   a. Describe Xerxes (called Ahasuerus in the Hebrew text). Review his actions toward Vashti, his advisers, the women in his harem, and the people of his country.

b. Describe Esther and Xerxes' relationship (Esther 2:17-18; 4:11; 5:3-8).

2. What unusual characteristics do you see in Esther? (Hint: See Esther 2:13-15 and 3:12-17.)

A Balanced Approach to Submission
3. Match the following words often used in explanations of submission to their proper definition. Use creative connecting lines.

Teachability	Open to instruction
Humility	Courteous regard or respect
Deference	To hold in high esteem
Obedience	Absence of pride or self-assertion
Respect	Carrying out instructions or orders
Responding	Surrendering or giving up
Yielding	Having a favorable reaction

4. **a.** Put a wife's submission in context by reading Ephesians 5:21–6:9. This passage explains how different believers are to be subject to one another "in the fear of Christ" (Ephesians 5:21). How are the following people challenged to show submission?

  ❦ Wives

  ❦ Husbands

  ❦ Children

  ❦ Fathers

❦ Slaves (employees)

❦ Masters (employers)

b. Which relationships use the word "obey"?

Which relationships do not?

Note: *"In the lists of rules for behavior patterns in the household the key thought in the New Testament is submission. There is a reciprocity between the members not found outside the New Testament."*[1]

5. What differences do you see in the challenge to husbands and wives versus masters and slaves?

a. Wife

Slave

b. Husband

Master

6. Which statement do you most agree with? Explain.

___ God wants me to do everything my husband desires no matter how resentful I feel.
___ God wants me to always obey my husband in everything and pray for a good attitude.

___ God would rather I do for my husband only what I can do with a cheerful, giving heart (See 2 Corinthians 9:7).

___ When I am unsure about the validity of my husband's desires, God wants me to pray and seek counsel.

Speaking the Truth in Love

7. Paraphrase Esther's response to Xerxes (Esther 5:8) in modern words, as though she were the wife of a high government official today.

8. How can a wise woman's words be like a goad in the sense of Ecclesiastes 12:11?

9. How did Esther show a submissive spirit toward her husband even as she challenged him or "goaded" him to better things? (Esther 7:3-4)

10. What other guidelines do you learn from Esther in Esther 4:12-17?

11. Highlight or draw flowers or stars, etc. in front of the best answers to the following sentence: *If a wife never challenges anything her husband says or does, she:*
    ❧ Pleases her husband
    ❧ Defrauds him
    ❧ Obeys the command to be submissive

- ❦ Becomes a nonperson
- ❦ Is not the helpmeet she should be
- ❦ Strengthens him
- ❦ Weakens him
- ❦ May cause him to stagnate and become self-centered
- ❦ Supports him

12. Check what is true of you right now.

___ I need to challenge my husband about something but am afraid.

___ I speak out too much and need to learn deference from Esther.

___ I need to remember to pray before I challenge my husband.

EXPLORING YOUR UNIQUENESS

13. Choose one activity:
    - ❦ Esther was honest about her emotional needs. At one point she even wept in the king's presence. Spend some time writing in your journal about an emotional need with which your husband helps you — or could help if you were bold enough to share honestly with him.
    - ❦ Enlarge on your answer to number 12. (Write a poem or meditation or draw a cartoon.) In what specific way can you work at a better balance between being too contentious and being too quiet?

INTERPRETING THE DATA

Biblical submission in marriage is not what most people think. It doesn't mean being servile or living life as a doormat. It doesn't mean that a woman is to always flatter her husband and do whatever pleases him at the moment. Sometimes it means gently goading him to better things.

One current Christian teaching on submission led a woman to believe that when God said she was to submit to her husband as to the Lord, He meant her husband would always be right. She thought submitting to her husband's every whim and desire without question was one of the most essential ingredients of making Christ the Lord of her life.

If husbands were always like Christ, then this way of relating would be proper. But we live in a fallen world, and husbands are fallible. A woman is an individual in her own right and has personal accountability to God. She has a mandate of integrity, a responsibility to help her husband see things he doesn't see. If a man understands this, he will be less defensive when his wife speaks. Her wisdom will enable both husband and wife to better understand the whole counsel of God.

Xerxes and his two wives, Vashti and Esther, are a picture of leadership and submission in an imperfect world. History tells us that this Persian king was a renowned builder who was generous with his wealth. But he also had a violent temper, so his leadership was spasmodic and often insensitive.

In Esther chapter 1, we learn that Xerxes' wife Vashti responded to her husband's failings with a proud spirit and public disobedience. But Esther's response to Xerxes, even when she challenged some of his decisions, was humble and deferential.

Her attitude made all the difference.

Speaking Gently

Sometimes women put on a show of submission when underneath they have a stubborn martyr-like spirit that is anything but what God desires. The woman who speaks her disagreement, but does it with a sensitive attitude, lays better groundwork for the future.

One man told his wife that he was thinking about using some real estate bonus money to buy a fancy sports car, in addition to the two cars the couple already owned. At first his wife said nothing. They often disagreed about the use of money, but she tried to be quiet unless the issues were important.

Then she found out that the job of their college-student son required him to travel across town several times a week. He didn't have a car and had to go by bus or taxi. His course work was heavy, and the time required to use public transportation made it difficult for him to keep up his grades. The wife felt her husband should be willing to set aside his own desires for a sports car and buy a car for their son. She didn't say anything for a while. But her unrest persisted, so she prayed about it. Finally she spoke to him.

"The more I hear about John's need for a car, the more I feel we should think about buying him one this year. I know you've been wanting the sports car for a long time. But perhaps you could find a used car for John and put the rest of the money in savings toward buying a sports car next year."

Because she spoke in a loving way and didn't push, her husband listened. He bought the car for John and was glad about the decision.

The word translated "submit" in Ephesians 5:21 is the Greek word *"hupotasso."* It means *to arrange under.* The whole Ephesian passage indicates that each person in a household submits for a greater purpose, that of inviting one another toward godly living. So a wife is to arrange herself under her husband as a support, asking herself what will encourage him toward wise and loving action. Sometimes God will lead her to goad or stimulate her husband in the manner of Ecclesiastes 12:11, "The words of the wise are like goads . . . given by one Shepherd."

The idea of goading conjectures pictures of pricking, stinging, or prodding mercilessly. But in ancient times, a man who was skillful with his oxen used his goad only as a wand, waving it gently in the air. He would walk backward in front of them, cajoling and praising, as the oxen leaned into their yokes and heaved, pulling the plow that turned the reluctant soil.

A woman can goad by nagging and pushing, bitterly quarreling and contending until her husband feels forced to do what she asks out of self-defense. She can goad him in a way that makes him wish they didn't live under the same roof.

But the best definition for a woman's proper goading would be "to quietly inspire." A wife who is submissive to her husband in the way that God desires will speak when the issues are important, but she will do it with gentleness and love. In some marriages, she will even move ahead of her husband, inspiring him and giving him solace through the difficult work he needs to do.

Providing a Mirror
Walter Wangerin says that a wife is meant to be a mirror the husband can count on, and vice versa. Who else can better help us to see ourselves as we really are? Each of us needs a trustworthy mirror that accurately reflects our flaws, as well as our virtues.

Sometimes a woman thinks submission means pretending she supports her husband when she really doesn't. If she continues this pretense, a time may come when she is so tired of pretending that she no longer desires to work at the marriage. Her lack of honesty could lead to breakup of the marriage.

A husband's unloving or unwise patterns of living cannot be ignored and pretended away. Sometimes we will need to goad (quietly inspire) our husbands in areas like the use of money, or the need to forgive, or the importance of a child's current need. At other times we must speak to them about dishonesty or other moral issues.

Even though a husband may think that he wants his wife to always follow his orders and never challenge anything he says or does, such a wife is not being the helper God meant her to be. She is deceiving her husband by giving him a distorted reflection of himself. She is defrauding him of opportunities to grow. She is encouraging him to become selfish. And she is squelching her own God-given skills.

Being Honest about Our Needs

Esther's situation was extreme. She was pleading with her husband for the lives of a nation. We will probably never find ourselves in such a dire circumstance. But we can learn from the way Esther brought her emotional needs to her husband. "How can I endure to see the calamity . . . how can I endure to see the destruction of my kindred?" (Esther 8:6, NASB)

One woman told her counselor that her husband felt most supported when she subordinated her needs to his. So she hid her feelings and tried not to talk about her interests. She lived this way for years. Finally she became so emotionally depleted that she couldn't cope any longer. She wanted to run.

The counselor showed her that she was using her rigid definition of submission as an escape. Because she didn't want her husband to disapprove of her in any way, she ignored her own needs and gave in to whatever he desired. Her "obedience" reduced their conflict. But it also reduced their intimacy.

A genuine submission involves bringing who we are and what we are feeling to our husbands: "This is who I am, and this is how it feels to be your wife and subject to all your decisions. Please help me."

In her book *The Measure of My Days*, psychologist Florida Scott-Maxwell says what we are afraid to say about the universal image of the ideal woman: "The selfless, tireless one, the rich giver and the meek receiver, with life-giving energy flowing like milk from the breast, costing her nothing is too, too much. Looked at in the grey light of daily living, the concept is the demand of the ravening child, and we cannot respond to such a claim in man or child."[2]

In Ephesians 5 the relationship of husband and wife is compared to the relationship of Christ and the church. It is Christ who meets the needs of the church, not the church who meets the needs of Christ. So it may be that God holds the husband more accountable to meet his wife's needs, than He does the wife to meet the husband's needs. Yet many a Christian husband expects his wife to meet all of his needs first. He may have it backward.

Finding the Balance

It would be easy to understand submission if submission meant always being quiet or always speaking our minds. But godly submission involves both speaking and not speaking. It involves bringing our needs to our husbands and yet not expecting them to meet all those needs. It means affirming as well as goading.

How can we find the balance of what is right at any given time? The key is learning how to put God first. Once we are married we create for ourselves a continual dilemma. We *want* to please our husbands. We feel that we *should* please our husbands. But we sense that pleasing a husband sometimes keeps us from being wholehearted toward God. Even the Apostle Paul observed this problem. He wrote, "But a married woman is concerned about the affairs of this world — how she can please her husband," (1 Corinthians 7:34b).

A woman once wrote the following letter in her diary:

"In what sense am I to put you first, my husband, you to whom I have made the most binding vows? What does this mean in everyday life? God is first.

If I can live with you being glad about your direction, accepting your flaws, content to not say anything about the way, for example, you are investing your time, I will. But if I keep experiencing unrest about a direction you are going or a decision you are making, I will take that as unrest from God, pray over it, and then respectfully speak to you about my concerns.

I am not responsible for what you do in the end, but I am responsible for my speaking. If I please you by pretending respect and agreement when inside I disagree, won't God someday confront me with my lack of integrity? If I say nothing, it may please you, but how can it please God?

Putting you first, after God in my life, means there will be times when I cannot please you the way you think you want to be pleased. But it also means that with the resources I have, I will serve you and do my best to meet your needs before I meet those of anybody else. And if I find myself resisting your leadership only because of pride and selfishness, I will ask God to enable me to follow you despite how I feel.

Being a loving and supportive woman is no easy thing. It takes wisdom and power from God Himself.

For Personal Meditation:
"The fruit of righteousness will be peace; the effect of righteousness will be quietness and confidence forever."

—Isaiah 32:17

PATHFINDING WITH YOUR HUSBAND (Essential!)

Choose one of the following:
1. Plan a special evening together. After a meal or a concert or something you enjoy, discuss the following questions:
   - How can a woman arrange herself under her husband in such a way that she is a strong support and a stimulus toward godly action? (The word "submit"—*hupotasso*—means "to arrange under."[3]
   - Discuss questions 4 and 5.
   - Share your journal entries from question 14.

2. Read the *Interpreting the Data* section together; discuss.

EXPLORING YOUR UNIQUENESS (Continued)

- Write about how you and your husband agree or disagree on the issue of submission.

GROWING TOGETHER
The Give and Take of a Good Marriage

LESSONS FROM THE MARRIAGE OF SARAH AND ABRAHAM

IMPORTANT: If at all possible, do this study with your husband.

Sarah bent over the steaming pot and lifted the ladle to her mouth. She frowned. "What did Hagar put in this soup?"

"I'm not sure, mistress," answered the servant who was kneading the bread for the day. "I wasn't here when she made it."

"Go get her at once."

The servant left, returned, and continued her bread-making. But another half-hour passed before Hagar appeared.

"Where have you been?" Sarah demanded. "The soup isn't fit to eat. And you haven't even started the washing."

Hagar's clenched fists went to her hips. Her dark eyes glittered. "I don't have time to mess with soup and dirty clothes; I have to get my rest."

Before Sarah could think what to reply, Hagar muttered low and spiteful, "You and your mighty airs. You can't even bear your husband a child."

Sarah's hand flew out and burned across Hagar's face. Hagar stood stunned. She cursed as her mistress, stalked out of the tent and straight to Abraham.

"It's all your fault." Sarah spat the words at her husband. "If you had treated Hagar like the servant she is, she wouldn't be acting like this now."

Abraham didn't know what to say. He felt half-guilty about the whole situation, but it had been Sarah's idea. "Deal with her however you wish," he sighed.

Sarah did. She abused Hagar so much that Hagar ran away. Later, feeling guilt, she apologized to her husband. "Perhaps I should have let you deal with her," she said.

"Never mind," he sighed, "if I were in your place, I might have done the same."

Sarah put her head on her husband's shoulder and felt the old comfort of his arms. Everything would be all right.

The Marriage

1. Read the following passages, and write a summary of what you learn about Sarah and Abraham's relationship in each passage.

❦ Genesis 12

❦ Genesis 16:1-6, 15

❦ Genesis 18:1-15

❦ Genesis 21:1-13

❦ Genesis 23:1-4, 17-20

2. Describe Abraham (*Optional reading:* Genesis 13:5-18 and Genesis 18:16-33).

3. Describe Sarah.

Note: *The name **Sarah** means "princess."*

4. **a.** How is your husband like, or not like, Abraham?

b. In what ways are you like, or not like, Sarah?

Deferring to One Another

5. Use the following resources to discover how Abraham and Sarah responded to each other's weaknesses.
a. Review Genesis 12:10-15.

How might Proverbs 31:12 apply to this incident?

b. Genesis 16:1-6
(Note: The phrase "voice of Sarah" in verse 2 can be translated the "weeping or thunder" of Sarah. According to *The Bible Knowledge Commentary*, "It was the legal custom of the day for a barren woman to give her maid to her husband as wife. Her suggestion was unobjectionable according to social custom."[1]

c. Genesis 18:9-15

6. The *New American Standard Version* translates Genesis 12:13, "Please say that you are my sister," and Genesis 16:2, "Please go in to my maid." The verb in each case is *na*, a primary particle of entreaty which means "I beg, I implore, I beseech." What does this show about Abraham's and Sarah's attitudes toward one another?

7. Sarah blamed Abraham for Hagar's contempt, and Abraham tried to diffuse the blame. What can blame do to a marriage? Cite an example in your marriage, or in someone else's.

8. Read 1 Peter 3:1-7. What stands out to you about a wife's responsibility?

   A husband's responsibility?

Mutual Suffering

9. The word used for Abraham's distress in Genesis 21:11 is *raa*. It means "afflict, do evil, grieve, or work calamity." Reread Genesis 21:8-13 and journal the thoughts Abraham might have had right after Sarah's advice to send Ishmael away.

10. Mike Mason in *The Mystery of Marriage* says, "There is no suffering like the suffering involved in being close to another person but neither is there any joy nor any real comfort at all outside of intimacy."[2]
    a. How have you suffered in your relationship?

    b. How has your husband suffered?

Mutual Reward

11. What words are repeated several times in Genesis 18:12-14 and Genesis 21:5-7?

Describe the mood of Genesis 21:1-7.

12. Compare what Sarah said when Isaac was born to what Rachel said when Joseph was born (Genesis 21:6-7 and 30:22-24).

EXPLORING YOUR UNIQUENESS

13. Choose *one* of the following to enter in your journal:
- ❧ What do you do when you sense that a resentment (or attitude of blame) is causing you to become bitter toward your husband? Chart three or more incidents. How would you like to change?
- ❧ Circle the area in which you would like to see a better give-and-take between you and your husband.
  - **a.** Courteous speech
  - **b.** Making allowances for weaknesses
  - **c.** Understanding each other's sufferings

  Write about a specific happening or need in the area you chose.
- ❧ Think of a mistake one of you has made. Draw something that shows how God turned it into good—or could turn it into good.
- ❧ Paste and caption an item in your journal to remind you of God's goodness in a home situation that could have brought harm.
- ❧ Write a poem.

INTERPRETING THE DATA

Artist and thinker Vincent Van Gogh once philosophized about love this way: "What kind of love was it I felt when I was twenty? . . . without asking anything in return, I only wanted to give, not to receive. Foolish, wrong, exaggerated, proud, for in love one must not only give but also take, and reversing it, one must not only take, but also give."[3]

He goes on to say that it is written that we are to love our neighbors as ourselves. To love either our neighbor or ourselves too much (or too little) falls short of balanced, healthy love.

It takes two to make a good marriage—both giving, both receiving, both listening to the other's needs, and both responding. It is a delusion to think that if a wife submits to her husband on every issue, and he does not do his part, the marriage will be a good one. The opposite is also true. If the husband leads with love and sacrifice, and the wife does little or nothing, the marriage still will not be a good one. If your marriage is to be what God intended, it will require the work of both partners.

Abraham and Sarah were individuals, yet one—bound up with one another: sending-receiving, receiving-sending, listening-responding, making allowances for each other. Their top priority in marriage was to be sensitive to the other's heart need, not to point out who was right and who was wrong.

Sarah's submission in 1 Peter 3:6 sounds simple, but in real life her submission issues were complex. Often the choices both she and Abraham faced were anything but black and white. When Abraham asked Sarah to say that she was his sister, she must have wondered if it was the right thing to do. She *was* Abraham's half sister, but she was also his wife. And yet, everywhere they traveled they heard terrifying stories about tribal leaders seizing beautiful women for their harems and killing their husbands. "Surely," Sarah must have thought, "it is the loving thing to do. I should say that I am his sister!"

And during the confusion of the Hagar-Ishmael affair, Abraham listened to and valued Sarah, remembering his own past failures. He was not judgmental of his wife.

Because theirs was a marriage of mutual give-and-take, it was a good marriage; not perfect, but alive and workable.

It Takes Two to Adapt

The marriage relationship is dynamic. It is always changing. Each spouse will need to make new changes this year that he or she didn't have to make last year. A new interest may change a comfortable schedule. A health problem may erupt. A different job may call for a change of place and friends. A new struggle in one spouse's faith could change the whole atmosphere.

The plains and valleys and hills of growth in our spouse may not coincide with our own. God was patient with Sarah's slow-growing faith. Abraham, the great man of faith, was also patient. Sarah had her own rate of spiritual growth. It was different from her husband's.

Sometimes a spouse will change in such a drastic way that he or she will seem like a different person. Pascal once commented on this phenomena in a certain marriage: "He no longer loves this person whom he loved ten years ago. I should think not; she is no longer the same, nor is he. He was young, and she too; she is quite different. He would perhaps love her now as she was then."[4] The natural reaction to this situation is to think divorce. A better way, however, is to view the change as an opportunity to learn to love in new ways. Professional counseling will often help both partners find ways to build on these changes and to make the marriage more firm than ever.

Sometimes a spouse will change for the better. One woman said that she needed to stop doubting her husband when he said he was growing in an area where he had been weak. When she refused to believe that he was changing, she imprisoned him in her disbelief.

It Takes Two to Show Consideration
A friend went to the doctor with severe anxiety symptoms. The doctor, a non-Christian, asked, "Where's your husband?"

She answered, "He's at work. We both try to be independent and not lean on each other too much."

The doctor shook his head. "You Christians don't do a very good job of taking care of each other, do you?"

C.S. Lewis says, "Christian writers have sometimes spoken of the husband's headship with a complacency to make the blood run cold. We must go back to our Bibles. The husband is the head of the wife just in so far as he is to her what Christ is to the Church. He is to love her as Christ loved the Church . . . and give his life for her." (Eph. 5:25)[5]

Lewis continues by saying that the crown of a husband's headship is his unwearying caring for a good wife in her sufferings, or his inexhaustible forgiving of a bad wife for her faults. One modern husband exhibits the kind of headship C.S. Lewis is talking about by being sensitive to his wife's daily emotional and physical needs. For example, if she looks tired around the eyes when she comes home from work, he brings in food from a Chinese restaurant they enjoy, or he orders pizza. When she cooks a meal, he declares it a minifeast. He is sensitive to the fact that coordinating dishes at supper is difficult. So he asks if he can help. If she prefers to work alone, he makes sure that she's not interrupted while cooking, and he comes to dinner as soon as she calls. These small considerations strengthen the marriage more each day.

Consideration also learns to speak the truth in love. Some husbands and wives boast that they can say anything to each other. "He knows that I love him. We can be free with one another."

"She understands."

Often, however, we use our liberty "to say anything" in obedience to our resentments. The art of love sometimes calls for being silent. And sometimes it involves knowing how to say what must be said so as not to wound, humiliate, or domineer.

It Takes Two to Forgive

There are times when all of us need to be the recipients of what the *King James* New Testament calls charity: love that we don't deserve.

Abraham and Sarah had many opportunities to love each other with "charity" and to forgive. Sarah could have refused to forgive Abraham for allowing her to be taken as Pharaoh's wife. She could have lived her life consumed with bitterness. But she chose not to. Abraham could have blamed Sarah for the heartbreak surrounding Ishmael. But he forgave.

A home that is Christ-centered will be one where there is an abundance of forgiveness: "Be ye kind one to another, tenderhearted, forgiving one another, even as God for Christ's sake hath forgiven you" (Ephesians, 4:32, KJV). When I remind myself of all the things for which God has forgiven me, it softens me toward my husband.

It is also helpful to deal with anger on a daily basis (Ephesians 4:26). One Sunday afternoon, as a woman and her husband were doing errands in preparation for a Christmas trip, both of them short-circuited. A heated argument, filled with blame, ensued. As they talked, the husband pointed out that the wife had been angry for several weeks.

From her point of view, she knew that she had been so busy with Christmas preparations that she had not taken time to deal with resentments. She had been sweeping them all into an invisible closet that she labeled "trying to accept my husband."

She thought about it. Later that afternoon she talked with her husband about how each resentment had begun. It was a healing time, which resulted in a positive Christmas trip, a trip that could have been disastrous. As a result, the woman resolved to be more diligent to deal with small resentments before going to bed each night. If we fail to do this, our anger can fester and turn into bitterness.

As the years of marriage go by and egos become more tender and bruised, we may avoid sharing our conflicts with each other because we are afraid of confrontation. But confrontation is often the sharp edge we need to cut through bitterness and to work through problems to the point of forgiveness.

Encouraging Give-and-Take

It takes two to make a good marriage. But how can wives encourage this mutuality? We can suggest to our husbands ways that they can help us—like asking them to be sensitive when we are preparing a meal. We can involve our husbands in discussion of marriage material like this book. We can agree on specific ways to generate more give-and-take. Then we can ask God to remind us both to deal with our anger each day and to focus more on the positives in our husbands.

Every marriage has its difficult seasons. It is during these seasons that commitment in marriage may seem like a prison. What commitment does, however, is to give you time—time to grow and time to make something better of your relationship. The word translated *pleasure* in Genesis 18:12 is *Eden*. Abraham and Sarah went through many trials in their marriage, but the Lord gave them *Eden* in old age. Nothing is too marvelous for our God.

For Personal Meditation:

"Two are better than one because they have a good return for their labor. For if either of them falls, the one will lift up his companion. But woe to the one who falls when there is not another to lift him up."

—Ecclesiastes 4:9-10 NASB

PATHFINDING WITH YOUR HUSBAND
(Much Needed!)

Choose one:
- ❦ If you were not able to do the study with your husband, read and discuss at least one section of *Interpreting the Data* together.

❧ Take a drive in a pretty area and end with a snack. Discuss: What does Ecclesiastes 4:9-10 mean in our marriage?

EXPLORING YOUR UNIQUENESS (Continued)

Choose one of the following:
❧ Journal about your discussion with your husband.
❧ Write a prayer for victory over any anger or bitterness. Then read Ephesians 4:25-27 in several translations. Write your favorite version in your journal or on a card for your desk or refrigerator.

EVERY MARRIAGE IS DIFFERENT
Summarizing Our Discoveries

LESSONS FROM THE MARRIAGES OF MARY AND JOSEPH AND PRISCILLA AND AQUILA

There He was at last. What was He doing? What in the world had He been thinking? The ache in her throat and chest slowly dissipated, and she gave in to the utter tiredness of three days of anxiety and sleeplessness.

She leaned against her husband, who strained to hear what the Boy was saying. Jesus seemed to be asking questions . . . no, it was He who was answering the questions. The teachers were talking to Him as though He were an equal.

Mary felt confused. "Should we correct Him?" she asked. Joseph only gave a bewildered shake of the head and drew her closer to him.

At last Jesus saw them and began moving their way. Unable to stand it any longer, Mary rushed toward her Son and grabbed Him by the shoulders. "I've been wild with panic. Why have You treated us this way?"

But Jesus' answer did nothing but add to her confusion. "My Father's business"? How could He expect them to know that He was going to stay in the temple to talk with the teachers?

On the way home Mary walked in a daze, not hearing, hardly seeing. And Joseph let her be, understanding her need to be alone with her thoughts. How grateful she was for her husband's protection—and his silence.

The Marriage
Read the following verses and then write a few sentences about:
1. The marriage of Mary and Joseph (Matthew 1:18–2:23; Luke 1:26–2:51).

2. The Importance of Being Yourself
a. What kind of person was Joseph? (Matthew 1:18-25; 2:13-23)

Note: In Mary and Joseph's time, the legal aspect of the marriage was the betrothal. Joseph had the right to claim Mary as his bride anytime after the betrothal.

b. Describe Mary. (Especially consider Luke 1:46-55, 2:19, and 2:51.)

c. How is Mary's individuality emphasized in the biblical account?

Note: The word *ponder* in Luke 2:19 means *to throw together*. It can be translated *discuss, consider,* or *reason.*[1]

3. Leadership and Submission
a. Star phrases that describe God's messages to Joseph. (Matthew 1:18-21; 2:13, 19-22).

Mary is wrong	Protect Mary
Take a new direction	Listen to your wife
Exhort your wife	Seek your own advancement
Love your wife	Get Mary under control
Be a leader	Other _____

b. How did Mary show a spirit of submission? Think through each scene:
The Annunciation

Joseph's initial decision not to take her as his wife (Matthew 1:19)

The journey to Bethlehem

The flight to Egypt

The return to Nazareth (Matthew 2:22-23)

c. Describe your husband's approach to leadership and your current response.

What would you like to do differently?

4. The Need to Listen
   a. Compare what God said to Abraham in Genesis 21:8-13 with Joseph's dream in Matthew 1:18-21.

   b. What do you notice about Joseph and Mary's parenting in Luke 2:21-24 and 2:41-52?

   c. One of the major causes of disunity in a marriage is the question of how to deal with the children. Why do you think Mary and Joseph seemed so united in their parenting?

d. What area of present or future parenting would you like to discuss or study with your husband in order to achieve more unity?

____ Method of discipline   ____ Boundaries in teen years

____ Dating   ____ Amount of individual time with each child

____ Devotions   ____ Amount of outside activities, lessons, sports

____ Curfew   ____ Friends

____ Respect   ____ Returning home after college

5. Love's joys and limitations

a. Consider Matthew 1:19 once more. When Joseph discovered that Mary was pregnant, he decided against making a public accusation with a demand for the full penalty of death. Instead he would use the lax divorce laws and give Mary the writing of divorcement in private with the accusation stated in a veiled way.[2] Why do you think he was so lenient with her?

b. Put yourself in Joseph's place. Write about the feelings and uncertainties he might have experienced. Or draw pictures to illustrate his dilemma.

c. Explain the power of unconditional love (1 Peter 4:8).

d. How would you like to apply 1 Peter 4:8 to your own marriage?

e. Mary had a good marriage that allowed her to depend on Joseph. But she was a widow for much of her life. What would Mary have to learn during her widowed years?

6. Oneness
a. What evidences of oneness do you see in the marriage of Mary and Joseph? (Luke 2:22, 39-40, 41-42)

b. Priscilla and Aquila
Note: This couple lived in Corinth 1½ to 2 years, then in Ephesus for 2 or 3. They probably returned to Rome when Nero took Claudius' place as emperor. They lived there for several years and then moved back to Ephesus.
   (1) Read:
      ❦ Acts 18
      ❦ 1 Corinthians 16:19 (written from Ephesus)
      ❦ Romans 16:3-5 (written to Christians in Rome after Priscilla and Aquila had been in Ephesus)
      ❦ 2 Timothy 4:19 (written to Timothy in Ephesus)

Comment on this marriage:

   (2) What kinds of things did Priscilla and Aquila do together?
      ❦ Acts 18:1-3

      ❦ Acts 18:24-26

      ❦ How does Paul describe them in Romans 16:3-4?

Note: Tentmakers were "either manufacturers of heavy cloth from goats' hair from which tents and other articles were made or [they were] leather workers."[3]

(3) Write a short vignette depicting Priscilla and Aquila's daily relationship. Start your story with the couple at work. Then have someone come to the door.

7. A Review

Pick one of the following themes and trace it through each of the marriages we have studied: *being yourself, leadership, oneness, listening, love, submission,* or *give-and-take.)*

For example, if you choose leadership, tell how each spouse led—the positives and the negatives. If you choose oneness, tell the ways each couple did or did not demonstrate oneness.

Theme you will trace: _____

Manoah and his wife

Isaac and Rebekah

Elizabeth and Zechariah

Nabal and Abigail

Jacob and Rachel

Hannah and Elkanah

Esther and Xerxes

Abraham and Sarah

EXPLORING YOUR UNIQUENESS

8. In your journal answer the following questions:

- ❦ Which marriage was most like yours? Explain.
  How was it different?
- ❦ What insights did you gain from this biblical marriage to help
  you in your own marriage?

INTERPRETING THE DATA

God's original plan for marriage was a beautiful thing: a synergism of
gifts and thinking, joy in giving and receiving, intimacy where there is
one but also two. God meant for the loving presence of a husband to
make the dailiness of life more bearable and the caring gentleness of a
wife to make troubles more tolerable. But we have fallen far short of
that ideal. The institution of marriage as we know it is a crystal vase
seared with hair-thin cracks, ready to shatter at a touch.

In their pace-setting book *The Mirages of Marriage*, Lederer and
Jackson say, "Year after year, in the United States, marriage has been
discussed in public print and private session with undiminished confusion and increasing pessimism. Calamity always attracts attention,
and in the United States the state of marriage is a calamity."[4]

Many Christian workers lead you to believe that the answers to marriage are simple. "Be kind, go to church, obey your husband, and everything will be all right." (This was the counsel a pastor actually gave to a couple who hadn't spoken to each other for several months.)

But our subtle layers of sin, our complex temperaments, our varied backgrounds, and our different weaknesses and strengths create too much of a maze for the working out of a lifelong relationship to be simple. And every child, relative, and friend poured into the marriage vase complicates matters even more.

Listening

We need continual dialogue—the kind of dialogue where each spouse takes turns emptying himself of himself so that he can hear the being and truth of the other; the kind of communication that is vulnerable and deals with resentments each day before the sun goes down. Every marriage is so different that unless we learn to talk and listen in these ways, we will never be able to discover what works for us.

Looking at models will help, but other people's marriages will never give all the answers you need. For example, many of us long for a marriage like Priscilla and Aquila's. But in real life that kind of marriage is rare.

Lederer and Jackson call Priscilla and Aquila's type of marriage the Stable-Satisfactory marriage. They say, "Such a harmonious and collaborative union has seldom been directly observed by the authors, and then only between elderly men and women who have been married for thirty or more years . . . The extraordinarily collaborative (marriage) usually results not only from experiences occuring solely *within* the limits of married life, but also from similarities in background, parental and family experiences, interests, ethnic lines, subcultures, and so forth—in other words, important basic shared experiences occurring before the marriage begins."[5]

So it is obvious that it will be impossible for most of us to achieve Priscilla and Aquila's degree of oneness. But if our basic values are the same, we can achieve the amount of oneness we need for a good marriage. Much will depend on quality dialogue.

Oneness

One husband and wife had the common goal of wanting a Christ-centered home. The husband suggested they invite people over once a week for dinner. They could talk with them and try to meet their needs over the meal. The wife was willing, but she found that cooking a meal for company every week with all the planning, the careful shopping in order to stay within the budget, getting the house ready and then cleaning up afterward was too much pressure. She worked outside the home, and they had small children. The couple discussed other methods of achieving their mutual goal of hospitality and decided that they would invite people for dessert instead of a meal. Because they could agree on this plan—and its goal—they were truly one.

In what important areas do you and your husband agree? Do you both desire to be good stewards of your money? To grow spiritually and mentally? To raise your children with a gentle but firm discipline? Whatever your common values, emphasize them. Concentrate on them. Come to an agreement on the methods you will use to put them into action. And your marriage will become increasingly shatterproof.

Headship and Submission

Oneness comes through give-and-take. It doesn't come through a husband's orders carried out implicitly by his wife, no matter how she feels. A marriage governed by commands and obedience sometimes plays out like the relationship between a parent and a child. At other times it looks like that of a master and a slave. Sometimes it assumes the feel of a general commanding a sergeant. And sometimes it even takes on the ways of host and parasite—one spouse draining the life from the other. None of these are God's design. We are partners, heirs together under the grace of God, moving along hand in hand.

We see this equality repeatedly in the marriages of the Bible. Manoah's wife was just as important as Manoah. The angel appeared to her, not to her husband. Esther had a pivotal place in her husband's life. He benefited from her initiative and courage. Elizabeth and Zechariah were given equal places of honor in God's sight. Both Mary and Joseph were essential in the parenting of Jesus—Mary to be the vessel, Joseph to be the protector.

In New Testament times, the word for submission carried with it the idea of the captains of two ships traveling in a fleet. When a crisis arose, one captain would choose to put himself under the other captain's authority. Both captains' ideas and needs were important, but at critical junctures, one yielded his right of decision to the other.

In the same way, there are crisis points in marriage when one person must lead. God has placed responsibility on the husband for these critical moments. A sensitive woman will know when that time comes.

Mary must have known it was one of those times when Joseph woke her in the middle of the night and said that they must flee to Egypt. She probably found it easy to follow him. Joseph was a pristine example of what it means for a husband to be a protector.

Being Yourself

Mary and Joseph worked well together. Their basic values were the same. But they were also distinct individuals. Mary had a secret place within herself where she withdrew to be alone with God. There, she was free to peruse the mysteries and treasures God gave her. And Joseph, a carpenter, spent much of his time creating, building, and dealing with people. Mary may have had little part in this portion of his life. But the gifts both Mary and Joseph brought to the marriage were like intricate etchings on two sides of a crystal vase, bringing interest and beauty to the whole. Their differences enlarged the capacity of the marriage.

Love

And what about the romance we long for? What about the yearning for love we hear in so much of our music? What about the holy passion to love and be loved that lives at the core of who we are? How we long for a bridegroom who will love us perfectly, touch and enhance our fragility! And how we dream of being able to love a man with a vibrant, unbreakable love. Perhaps that dream is a foreshadowing of what we will experience when we become the bride of Christ.

Meanwhile God says that every Christian receives in Christ the seed of a sincere love for others. He commands us to nurture that seed until we grow to "love one another deeply, from the heart" (1 Peter 1:22-23). God wouldn't have commanded such a thing if it were not possible. He will help us.

Oh God, "may my desires be enlarged and my hopes emboldened that I may honor Thee by my entire dependency and the greatness of my expectation."[6]

"[Thou], who hast consecrated the state of Matrimony to such an excellent mystery . . . Look mercifully upon these Thy servants."[7]

PATHFINDING WITH YOUR HUSBAND
(A Mutual Summing Up)

Choose one of the following:

1. Read the *Interpreting the Data* section and share thoughts. (Consider doing this with another couple.)

2. Discuss one of the following quotes:
   * "Even for their own sakes [human] loves must submit to be second things if they are to remain the things they want to be. In this yoke lies true freedom; they 'are taller when they bow.' "[8] God alone deserves to be our first love.
   * "Marriage . . . is a crystal vase seared with hair-thin cracks, ready to shatter at a touch."

3. Discuss several parenting issues outlined in question 4d on page 76.

4. Take a weekend retreat alone with your husband.
   —Evaluate together the current state of your marriage.
   —Discuss parenting issues like those mentioned in question 4d.
   —Set marriage and family goals for the coming year.

EXPLORING YOUR UNIQUENESS (Continued)

Review the Personal Meditation quotes. Copy any missing ones into your journal and use them for your devotional times in the coming weeks.

INTRODUCTION

Consider the following guidelines and hints for leading this study:

1. "Never, never, never criticize your husband in public," a godly woman once counseled those she taught. As you lead this study and seek to guide your group of women in an honest discussion of marriage, encourage them to maintain supportive attitudes toward their husbands—not to be "Pollyannaish," but loving and discreet. Your wise example will help set the tone of each discussion.

2. If someone has a marital problem that she needs to discuss in detail, suggest meeting in twos for sharing and prayer. You may also want to have a good Christian counselor in mind in case it becomes evident that a couple needs counseling.

3. The section entitled *PathFinding with Your Husband* may be the most important section in each chapter. It takes two to make a marriage. Encourage the women to make a special effort to work on their study early in the week so they will have a chance to work in one of the suggested discussion times with their husbands.

4. In order to stimulate the husband's interest, it is recommended that you schedule two "discussion parties" for husbands and wives—one after the third lesson and one after the sixth. (See pages to 99-101.)

5. Each session will contain a question to brainstorm at the beginning of the group discussion. This will stimulate thinking and help each person feel that her contribution is important. (And it is!!!) You will need a bulletin board with 3 x 5 cards and tacks, or a large sheet of paper and a broad felt-tip pen. Allow five to ten minutes for this activity.

6. Your discussion of the Bible study material will be more stimulating if some of your questions are different in wording but the same in content as the ones your group has already studied. Choose from the questions given in the Leader's Guides or make up your own, being sure that your main questions are broad enough to cover most of a section.

7. Other hints: star questions in the *Lessons from the Marriage of . . .* section that you want to be sure to discuss. Use general questions that will encourage more people to speak. For example: What stood out to you in the personal study section? Do you have any comments or questions about the narrative section? Does anybody else have a thought you would like to share on this question?

8. Keep in mind that the goal of the *Exploring Your Uniqueness* section is to encourage each woman to begin a journal in which she can sort out her own thoughts: chart husband and wife personality differences, pray, confess, write down new insights or personally helpful Scriptures and do other creative activities related to her marriage.

9. Allow at least two hours for each session (with fun refreshments if possible). If you have more than eight women in your study, you may need to add another half hour or divide into subgroups.

GIVING YOUR SPOUSE A NAME

OBJECTIVE: To help group members see the value of their unique personalities.

PERSONAL PREPARATION:
1. Complete chapter 1.
2. Spend some time reading about Manoah's time in a commentary.
3. Read item 5 under GROUP DISCUSSION below, and choose the questions you would like to use. Add others.
4. Flip through several women's magazines and cut out pictures of different kinds of women: athletic, intellectual, sedate, dramatic, etc.
5. Buy spiral notebooks for everyone to use as journals.
6. As you work on the schedule for your Bible study meetings, schedule two "discussion-party" sessions to include husbands and wives (one after chapter 3 and one after chapter 6).

GROUP DISCUSSION:
1. Begin by reading Ephesians 5:31-33. Then use these verses as a guide for your opening prayer.
2. Ask each group member to choose a picture from your clippings that shows something of her personality. Ask each woman to explain her choice.
3. Explain brainstorming to your group members: You will be giving them a question or a problem. Then you want them to share any idea that comes to mind. Emphasize the fact that the most important rule for effective brainstorming is to *never criticize or make a value judgment on anybody's idea.* Sometimes the zaniest ideas will turn out to be the most helpful. Ask a "secretary" to write each idea on a 3 x 5 card and tack it to the bulletin board. *Brainstorming Question for Session 1:* How would you illustrate or define the concept of unity in diversity?
4. Have the group summarize the story of Manoah and his wife. Then share this quote from the Jewish historian Josephus. "There was one Manoah who was without dispute the principal person of his country. He had a wife celebrated for her beauty and excelling her contemporaries. . . . He was fond of his wife to a degree of madness."[6]

5. Questions for guiding your discussion by sections:
   - ❧ *Everyone Is Someone:* In what ways is the importance of a name emphasized in this chapter? Discuss question 3.
   - ❧ *Her Personality; His Personality:* What kind of personality did Manoah's wife have? How would you describe Manoah?
   - ❧ *How They Worked Together:* How did Manoah and his wife encourage each other? How is your marriage like this one?
   - ❧ *Interpreting the Data:* What stood out to you in this section? Why is it important that we be ourselves in our marriages?
   - ❧ Who would like to share something from your *Exploring Your Uniqueness* project or from your discussion with your husband?
6. Distribute the spiral notebooks and ask the women to paste or staple their *Exploring Your Uniqueness* assignment on the second page, the picture they chose on the third, etc. Suggest ideas for journal organization.

LOOKING FOR ANSWERS IN PRAYER:
Spend time in group prayer praising God. Talk to God about your personal strengths and weaknesses. Then thank Him for the balance of opposites in your husband.

LIVING WITH A PASSIVE HUSBAND

OBJECTIVE: To help the women understand the kind of loving leadership God designed a husband to exercise so that she will better understand her own responsibilities.

PERSONAL PREPARATION:
1. Read Genesis 24:1–28:9 in one sitting in order to understand the full scope of Isaac and Rebekah's life together.
2. Complete chapter 2.
3. Read item 3 under GROUP DISCUSSION below, and choose the questions you would like to use. Add others on points in the study that were meaningful to you.

GROUP DISCUSSION:
1. Begin your second session with brainstorming using the following question:
   What did God mean when He said the husband was to be the "head of the wife"? Throw out as many interpretations as you can think of, yours and others you have heard.
2. Have the group share the highlights of Isaac and Rebekah's story without referring to their study.
3. Questions for guiding your discussion by sections:
   a. *Married to an Opposite.* How did Isaac and Rebekah's differences complement one another? Share your answers to number 4.
   b. *The Beginnings of Conflict.* How did Isaac's kind of leadership cause problems?
   c. *How Isaac and Rebekah Failed to Work Together.* Explain Rebekah's dilemma when she heard that Isaac was going to give the patriarchal blessing to Esau. What kind of choices do you have when your husband seems set on doing something unwise, or even wrong?
   d. *A Godly Headship.* Describe God's plan for the kind of leadership He wants a husband to provide.

   e. *Interpreting the Data.* What thought would you like to discuss from the *Interpreting the Data* section? How do you understand the difference between contention and a godly persevering with your husband?

4. Ask the women to share something that was helpful to them in their discussion time with their husbands (*Pathfinding*).

5. Encourage them to share something that they charted, drew, or wrote in their journals. (You may also want to discuss the possibility of working together on memorizing your Personal Meditation quotations.)

LOOKING FOR ANSWERS IN PRAYER:

Hand out 3 x 5 cards or sheets from a colored notepad and ask each person to write down a prayer request. Have them put these requests in a basket (without signing them if they wish). Ask each person to draw a prayer request. Then spend some time praying over the requests together. Encourage the women to keep the request they drew, and continue to pray about it through the week.

THE TWO WHO BECAME ONE

OBJECTIVE: To help group members understand the meaning of genuine oneness and begin to take steps toward a greater oneness in their own marriages.

PERSONAL PREPARATION:

1. Read Luke 1 several times. Complete chapter 3.
2. Use a commentary to research the priesthood in New Testament times and the problem of infertility.
3. Read the questions in number 2 under GROUP DISCUSSION, and mark the ones you would like to use. Add others.

GROUP DISCUSSION:

1. Make your final plans for a husband and wife get-together that you will have at your next session.
   a. Study the plan for couples' discussion party on pages 99-100. Make any adjustments to the outline that will make the party more appropriate to your group.
   b. Appoint someone to send invitations to each couple represented in your group.
2. Use the following question for today's brainstorming:
   In what areas or situations might a husband and wife have difficulty in achieving oneness? (Get as many answers as you can.)
3. Discussion questions:
   a. *The Same Values.* Describe Elizabeth and Zechariah. Share your answer to question 4.
   b. *Elizabeth's Needs.* What kinds of traumas did Elizabeth experience in the first part of her marriage? If a wife and husband were one, what would their relationship be like during difficult times?
   c. *Zechariah's Needs.* Explain Zechariah's needs during and after the temple experience. Share your answers to questions 10 and 12.
   d. *Mutual Support.* Explain your concept of mutual support.
   e. *Interpreting the Data.* Which definition of oneness has been your definition? What was most helpful to you in this teaching section?

f. Share something that stood out to you in your time with your husband. (If your group is not getting this done, have them try approaching it spontaneously, suggesting discussion when their husband seems to be in the mood. Also suggest that they consider the Pathfinding activities of all the chapters as resources for the future.)

LOOKING FOR ANSWERS IN PRAYER:
Ask the women to update everybody on praises and answers to prayer. Then pray about current needs.

SURVIVING A DIFFICULT MARRIAGE

OBJECTIVE: To broaden the women's understanding of dialogue and help them begin to improve communication in their marriages.

PERSONAL PREPARATION:
1. Complete chapter 4.
2. Read item 2 under GROUP DISCUSSION below, and choose the questions you would like to use. Add or substitute your own questions.

GROUP DISCUSSION:
1. Brainstorm: What factors contribute to good dialogue?
2. Discussion questions:
   a. *Nabal's and Abigail's Personalities.* What was Nabal like? Describe Abigail. Describe the strengths and weaknesses of the marriage they created.
   b. *The Marriage's Personality.* Share your number 6 exercise. List and discuss different ways a woman can respond to a husband who doesn't seem to want to listen. How do you think Abigail responded? Discuss number 8.
   c. *Genuine Listening and Its Benefits.* Compare the way David listened with the way Nabal listened. Help your group members discuss and share insights from their work on questions 10 through 12.
   d. *Interpreting the Data.* What kind of talking and listening is necessary in a marriage to prevent the partners from feeling alone? Explain your understanding of Reuel Howe's definition of dialogue (p. 39).
   e. Tell something about your discussion with your husband.

LOOKING FOR ANSWERS IN PRAYER:
Close with silent prayer. Ask each woman to pray about a difficult area of communication with her husband. Then pray aloud through the *ACTS* acrostic: Adoration, Confession, Thanksgiving, Supplication.

LONGING FOR LOVE

OBJECTIVE: To examine the love in our marriages and then focus on God as the only one who loves perfectly.

PERSONAL PREPARATION:
1. Complete chapter 5.
2. Read Genesis 28:6–33:20: the marriage of Jacob and Rachel.
3. Decide on your discussion questions using the guide below.

GROUP DISCUSSION:
1. Brainstorm the following question: What is love?
2. Discussion questions:
   a. *Surveying the Marriages of Rachel and Hannah.* Describe the marriage of Rachel and Jacob. The marriage of Hannah and Elkanah.
   b. *Growing in Love.* What evidences of romantic love do you see in Rachel and Jacob's story? Share answers to number 5. Discuss the statement in number 8.
   c. *Realizing We Need More.* When can love become a curse as suggested in number 9? What evidences of a mature love do you see in the Hannah and Elkanah story? Share answers to questions 9, 10, and 13. How would you like to experience God's love this next week?
   d. *Interpreting the Data.* What stood out to you in this section about human love? About God's love?
   e. Read the last two paragraphs of this section aloud. Invite reactions.
   f. Share something from your journaling activity or from a discussion with your husband about one of the topics in this book.

LOOKING FOR ANSWERS IN PRAYER:
Pray spontaneously, each woman asking according to her need. End by having the group pray through Ephesians 3:14-21. Ask group members to select one phrase or request from that prayer and pray it for some other member of the group.

KNOWING WHEN TO TAKE A STAND

OBJECTIVE: To help your group understand submission with its proper biblical balance and begin work on this balance.

PERSONAL PREPARATION:
1. Read the whole Book of Esther. (Make notes.)
2. Complete chapter 6 in the study.
3. Decide on your discussion questions.

GROUP DISCUSSION:
1. Make plans for the Discussion Party coming up. See sample plans on page 101. Adjust these plans in whatever way seems appropriate for your group. Send invitations to each couple. Appoint a leader for the discussion party.
2. Start your discussion with a brainstorming question like: "What is submission?" or "What explanations of submission have you heard?"
3. Discussion questions:
   a. *The Marriage.* Describe Xerxes' personality. Describe Esther.
   b. *A Balanced Approach to Submission.* What do we learn about different kinds of submission in Ephesians 5:21–6:9? Which definition of submission in question 6 do you like best? Why?
   c. *Speaking the Truth in Love.* What were some of the things that Esther did to encourage her husband to listen to her even when she was challenging his actions? Which extreme do you tend to lean toward—being too quiet or speaking too much? Explain.
   d. *Interpreting the Data.* What was most helpful to you in this section? What questions do you still have? What do you think is the purpose of God's command for marriage partners to each submit to the other?
   e. Share something from a discussion with your husband.

LOOKING FOR ANSWERS IN PRAYER:
Divide into groups of three or four. Pray about current needs.

GROWING TOGETHER

OBJECTIVE: To help each woman see the importance of mutual give-and-take in marriage. To focus especially on dealing with anger and change.

PERSONAL PREPARATION:

1. Read Genesis 12–23. Make an outline of the events in Abraham's life.
2. Complete chapter 7 in the study.
3. Decide on your discussion questions.

GROUP DISCUSSION:

1. Brainstorm the following question: What word or phrase would you use to describe a marriage in which one partner does most of the giving?
2. Discussion questions:
   a. *The Marriage.* How would you describe the marriage of Sarah and Abraham?
   b. *Deferring to One Another.* Share your answers to numbers 7 and 8.
   c. *Mutual Suffering.* How did Abraham and Sarah suffer in their marriage? Share your imaginative vignettes or meditations from number 9. Discuss Mike Mason's quote in question 10.
   d. *Mutual Reward.* Share something from your **Exploring Your Uniqueness** activity.
   e. *Interpreting the Data.* What stood out to you in this section? How can we deal with bitterness? In what areas of your life are you now dealing with change? How can you approach these changes in ways that strengthen your marriage?

LOOKING FOR ANSWERS IN PRAYER:

Lead the entire group in guided prayer. Have them pray silently as you guide their prayers with the statements below:

1. Talk to the Lord about changes now occurring in your marriage. Ask His help in using that change as an avenue for growth.
2. Pray about times when you find it difficult to love your husband. Ask for God's perspective and love.

3. Talk to God about forgiveness in a particular area of your relationship. If you are able, pray a prayer of personal forgiveness toward your husband.
4. Pray for any other needs that come to mind.

EVERY MARRIAGE IS DIFFERENT

OBJECTIVE: To review the major themes of this book. To help each woman make applications for her own "one of a kind" marriage.

PERSONAL PREPARATION:
1. Complete chapter 8 of this study.
2. Review the "Interpreting the Data" section of the other seven chapters.
3. Decide on Discussion Questions.

GROUP DISCUSSION:
1. Ask for explanations of each major theme of this book: Individuality, Leadership, Oneness, Dialogue, Love, Submission.
2. Discussion questions:
   a. *The Importance of Being Yourself.* How is Mary's individuality brought out in the biblical account?
   b. *Leadership and Submission.* Describe Joseph's leadership and Mary's response.
   c. *The Need to Listen.* In what areas of parenting do you and your husband have difficulty agreeing (4d)? Discuss helpful resources.
   d. *Love's Joys and Limitations.* Discuss the teachings of 1 Peter 4:8 and 1 John 4:7-8 as they apply to your own marriage.
   e. *Oneness.* Describe the marriage of Priscilla and Aquila.
   f. Share answers to numbers 7 and 8.
   g. *Interpreting the Data.* What are your questions or comments?
   h. *Personal Application.* Share something from your journal.

LOOKING FOR ANSWERS IN PRAYER:
Have each woman write a long-term prayer request for her marriage on a card. Exchange cards. Then pray for each other. Keep the cards as a reminder to keep on praying for the person whose name you drew—even after this series of studies has ended. If your group is breaking up at this point, agree to meet again in one month to discuss the progress in your marriages and to pray for each other once again.

COUPLES' DISCUSSION PARTY, NO. 1
To be held after Group Session 3

7:00—People arrive. (Give out name tags.)

7:15—Icebreaker: Everyone sits in a circle. Hostess gives each person twelve pennies. The first participant tells something he, or she, has never done. He may say, for example, "I have never mowed a lawn," or "I didn't go to kindergarten." This participant then has to give up one penny for every person in the room who can say, "I've never done that either." Continue around the circle with everyone mentioning something they have never done. The goal is to keep as many pennies as possible. The person who still has pennies when everyone else has lost theirs is the winner.

7:45—Refreshments (Several women provide their favorite dessert or snack.)

8:10—Leader of study gives general outline of what the women are studying. Keep the tone nonthreatening.

8:15—Someone else, a husband if possible, explains the discussion part of the evening:

　　a. "We will divide into two groups to discuss some questions that touch on what our wives have been studying."

　　b. "Two men will pick a question apiece from the basket, and two women will do the same thing. All the men will then adjourn to another room and discuss their two questions. Then each group will pick a spokesperson to share his or her comments and answers with the whole group 15 minutes later."

Questions to use:

(1) Consider this quote: "It is as if the marriage license is construed as a sculptor's license, giving each spouse the warrant to chisel away until the other becomes the spit and image of the sculptor."

　　a. Why do you think this happens?

　　b. What are the dangers of this kind of thinking?

(2) What makes a man feel accepted?

(3) What makes a woman feel accepted?

(4) How would you define oneness in marriage?

8:30—The leader invites people back to a single group and initiates a reporting session.

8:55—Have someone close the evening with prayer. Be sure to end by 9:00.

This format is tried and proved. The key is to keep the evening light-hearted and nonthreatening.

COUPLES' DISCUSSION PARTY, NO. 2
To be held after Group Session 6

7:00—People arrive. Introduce any newcomers.

7:15—Icebreaker: Before the party, make a list of famous couples (biblical, political, literary, etc.). You will need as many couples as there are people at the party. Then write the famous couples' names on cards.

As guests arrive, place the name of a couple on the back of each person. Don't let them see what is on the nametag. When several couples have arrived, ask them to begin questioning each other to try to discover the name of their couple. They can only ask questions that can be answered, "Yes or No."

Give a first and second prize to the first two people who guess their famous couple.

7:45—Refreshments (Several women supply a favorite treat.)

8:10—One person gives a quick summary of what the women have studied together since the previous couples' party.

8:15—The leader for the evening announces that men and women will be discussing the same two questions in separate groups. The leader then hands out copies of the questions, instructs each group where to hold its meeting and when to return with a report.

Discussion questions:
   a. What does a good listener do and not do?
   b. My husband/wife was a great help to me when. . . .

8:30—The leader invites people back to a central area and initiates a reporting session. Allow opportunity for everyone to make a personal comment about the second question.

8:55—Closing prayer. (Ask someone ahead of time to be prepared.)

9:00—Everyone is free to leave or linger, as they choose.

ENDNOTES

Chapter 1

1. Irving Stone, *Dear Theo* (New York: New American Library, 1937), p. 47.
2. David Keirsey and Marilyn Bates, *Please Understand Me* (Del Mar, Calif.: Prometheus Nemesis Books, 1978), p. 68.
3. Jeremy Taylor, quoted by Mike Mason, *The Mystery of Marriage* (Portland, Ore.: Multnomah Press, 1985), p. 23.
4. Walter Wangerin, *As for Me and My House* (Nashville: Thomas Nelson Publishers, 1987), p. 45.
5. Harry and Bonaro Overstreet, *The Mind Goes Forth* (New York: W.W. Norton & Co., Inc. 1956), p. 38.
6. Flavius Josephus, Trans. by William Whiston, *The Complete Works of Josephus* (Grand Rapids, Michigan: Kregel Publications, 1960), pp. 118–19.

Chapter 2

1. David Keirsey and Marilyn Bates, *Please Understand Me* (Del Mar, Calif.: Prometheus Nemèsis Books, 1978), p. 68.
2. John F. Walvoord, Roy B. Zuck, editors, *The Bible Knowledge Commentary* (Wheaton, Ill.: Victor Books, 1985), p. 72.
3. Charles F. Pfeiffer, Everett F. Harrison, editors, *Wycliffe Bible Commentary* (Chicago: Moody Press, 1962), pp. 29–30.
4. Bob Moorehead, *The Husband Handbook* (Brentwood, Tenn.: Wolgemuth & Hyatt Publishers, Inc., 1990), p. 8..
5. Merle Shain, *Courage My Love* (Toronto: Bantam Books, 1989), p. 76.
6. George MacDonald, *Proving the Unseen* (New York: Ballantine Books, 1989), pp. 2–3.

Chapter 3

1. Henri Daniel-Rops, *Daily Life in the Times of Jesus* (New York: New American Library of World Literature, 1962), pp. 365, 367.
2. James I. Packer, Merrill C. Tenney, William White, *The Bible Almanac* (Nashville: Thomas Nelson Publishers, 1980), p. 441.
3. Packer, Tenney, White, *The Bible Almanac*, p. 412.
4. Howard and Charlotte Clinebell, *The Intimate Marriage* (New York: Harper & Row, 1970), p. 19.
5. Lois Wyse, *Love Poem for the Very Married* (Cleveland: World Publishing Co., 1967), p. 51.

Chapter 4

1. Charles F. Pfeiffer, Everett F. Harrison, editors, *Wycliffe Bible Commentary* (Chicago: Moody Press, 1962), p. 290.

2. Henri Nouwen, *The Road to Daybreak* (New York: Image Books, 1988), p. 167.

3. Walter Wangerin, *As for Me and My House* (Nashville: Thomas Nelson, Inc., 1987), p. 166.

4. Howard J. Clinebell, Jr. and Charlotte H. Clinebell, *The Intimate Marriage* (New York: Harper & Row, 1970), p. 33.

5. Reuel L. Howe, *The Miracle of Dialogue* (New York: The Seabury Press, 1963), p. 4.

6. Wangerin, *As for Me and My House*, p. 168.

7. Maxim Gorki, *The Lower Depth* (Boston: International Pocket Library, 1906), p. 99.

8. Matthew Henry, John Gill, Arthur Pink, *An Exposition of I and II Samuel* (MacDill AFB, Fla.: MacDonald Publishing Company, undated), p. 238.

9. Howe, *The Miracle of Dialogue*, p. 57.

10. Arthur Bennett, editor, *The Valley of Vision* (Bungay, Suffolk: The Chaucer Press, 1975), p. 116.

11. Martin Buber, *The Way of Response* (New York: Schocken Books, 1966), p. 83.

Chapter 5

1. Howard J. Clinebell, Jr. and Charlotte H. Clinebell, *The Intimate Marriage* (New York: Harper and Row Publishers, 1970), p. 75.

2. Charles F. Pfeiffer, Everett F. Harrison, editors, *Wycliffe Bible Commentary* (Chicago: Moody Press, 1962), p. 275.

3. Al Novak, *Hebrew Honey* (Houston, C&D International, 1987), pp. 22–23.

4. John F. Walvoord, Roy B. Zuck, editors, *The Bible Knowledge Commentary* (Wheaton, Ill.: Victor Books, 1985), p. 76.

5. C.S. Lewis, *The Four Loves* (New York: Harcourt Brace Jovanovich, 1960), pp. 74–75.

6. Walvoord, *The Bible Knowledge Commentary*, p. 77.

7. Thomas Merton, *No Man Is an Island* (San Diego: Harcourt Brace Jovanovich, 1955), p. 10.

8. Octavio Paz, *The Labyrinth of Solitude: Life and Thought in Mexico* (New York: Grove Press, Inc., 1961), p. 41.

Chapter 6

1. Colin Brown, editor, *The New International Dictionary of New Testament Theology, Vol. 3* (Grand Rapids, Mich.: Zondervan Publishing House, 1971), p. 929.
2. Florida Scott-Maxwell, *The Measure of My Days* (New York: Penguin Books, 1968), pp. 101–2.
3. Robert L. Thomas, editor, *New American Standard Exhaustive Concordance of the Bible* (Nashville: Holman Bible Publishers, 1981), pp. 1687, 1689.

Chapter 7

1. John F. Walvoord, Roy B. Zuck, editors, *The Bible Knowledge Commentary* (Wheaton, Ill.: Victor Books, 1985), p. 56.
2. Mike Mason, *The Mystery of Marriage* (Portland, Ore.: Multnomah Press, 1985), p. 72.
3. Irving Stone, editor, Vincent Van Gogh, *Dear Theo* (New York: New American Library, 1937), p. 67.
4. Blaise Pascal, Arthur H. Beattie, Editor, *Selections from the Thoughts* (Northbrook, Ill.: AHM Publishing Corporation, 1965), pp. 13–14.
5. C.S. Lewis, *The Four Loves* (New York: Harcourt Brace Jovanovich, 1960), p. 148.

Chapter 8

1. Robert L. Thomas, editor, *New American Standard Exhaustive Concordance* (Nashville: Holman Bible Publishers, 1981), p. 1642.
2. Charles F. Pfeiffer, Everett F. Harrison, editors, *The Wycliffe Bible Commentary* (Chicago, Moody Press, 1962), p. 932.
3. Pfeiffer, Harrison, *Wycliffe Commentary*, p. 1158.
4. William J. Lederer and Dr. Don D. Jackson, *The Mirages of Marriage*, (New York: Norton, 1968), p. 13.
5. Lede. - Jackson, *Mirages of Marriage*, pp. 130, 133.
6. Arthur L. nett, editor, *The Valley of Vision* (Edinburgh: The Banner of Truth Trust, 1975), p. 116.
7. From "The Form of Solemnization of Matrimony" in *The Book of Common Prayer*.
8. C.S. Lewis, *The Four Loves* (New York: Harcourt Brace Jovanovich, 1960), p. 166.
9. C.S. Lewis, editor, *George MacDonald, 365 Readings* (New York: Macmillan Publishing Company, 1947), p. 58.